Dedication

To the children of our community
in memory of
the 1.5 million Jewish children
murdered during the Holocaust

So that they will know
and not forget . . .

In Our Midst

How The Holocaust Touched
One American Community

Keshet Press
Binghamton, NY
1997

Keshet Press
9 Riverside Dr.
Binghamton, NY 13905-4611
(607) 723-7355

First edition published 1997
Printed in the United States of America

Library of Congress Cataloguing-in-Publication Data

In our midst / edited by Lance J. Sussman and Mary Rose.
p. cm.
Includes bibliographical references and index summary.
A compilation of first person accounts by survivors and
witnesses of the Jewish Holocaust.
        ISBN 1-883058-37-6 (hard cover)
        ISBN 1-883058-36-8 (soft cover)
1. Holocaust, Jewish (1939-1945) Personal narratives -
        juvenile literature.
2. Holocaust, Jewish (1939-1945) Personal narratives .
3. World War II, 1939-1945 - Jews. Sussman, Lance
        Jonathan.
4. Rose, Mary.
D804.34.15   1997   96-37875
940.53'18-dc21   CIP
                             AC

Editors' Note:

The illustrations in this book were primarily chosen for their content. Extensive efforts have been made to generate quality reproductions of original photographs and drawings as a matter of historical record. The physical size of some of the illustrations have been changed to highlight relevant details or improve the quality of our book's design.

Cover Art. Line drawing, interior skyview of Holocaust Memorial, Temple Israel, Vestal, New York.

Stephanie Horowitz, artist . . . 1997

Table of Contents

— Foreword

The Holocaust, the common name by which we call the planned murder of six million Jews in Europe between 1941 and 1945, is today more than fifty years in the past, and part of a European history that seems very far away from young people in the United States.

However, despite its belonging to the past, and despite its having taken place in geographical locations far away and in cultures very different from our own, it has a pressing relevance for all Americans, especially those who will inherit the future. Though almost every major political, ethical, cultural and religious question looks different after Auschwitz, I would stress here only one point for consideration, namely, the crucial issue of "bystanderism." The killing of Jews and others was, of course, carried on by the Nazis and their many allies, and they must bear the primary responsibility of the monstrous evil that occurred. Yet, this evil happened, at least in part, because many otherwise good people looked on indifferently, preoccupied with their own problems or afraid to "become involved," and let those who were evil do the deed. Evil only succeeds because good men and women let it.

"Bystanders" were not only those who lived in Germany or France or Poland, and who saw their Jewish and other neighbors dragged away by the Gestapo, or who watched from the sidelines as ghettos were created in the cities of Europe and concentration camps sprang up over the countryside, or who stood by as millions were herded like animals into dark, cold, unsanitary trains for deportation to "the East" which meant extermination in specially created death camps in Poland. "Bystanders" were also those who, from afar, knew at least the outlines of what was happening and did nothing those who, though separated from events by an ocean, did not raise their voice in protest; those in safe democratic lands who did not push for changes in national emigration policy that would have saved lives; those who did not wish to hear the pained voices of orphaned children and destitute teenagers; and those who simply preferred to turn inward and ignore this immense human tragedy. As the wise eighteenth-century English political thinker, Edmund Burke, already knew: "The only thing necessary for the triumph of evil is for good men to do nothing."

Every young person who reads this book should know that today the world is still full of tragedy, both at home and abroad. That the world, your world, needs your intelligence, your caring, your involvement. Modern communications make it impossible for you to say, "I didn't know." It is your obligation to make sure no one else says, "you didn't care."

Steven T. Katz

— Preface

I first became aware of the Holocaust as a child playing in my grandmother's house. One day I was busy exploring the inner recesses of the large buffet in her dining room when I found an old cardboard ring box with German written on it in gold letters. I was surprised to find a lock of hair inside the tiny treasure chest instead of a piece of jewelry. Oma, as I called my grandmother, did not answer me when I asked her about my discovery.

Later that day my mother explained to me that the curl of hair belonged to her best friend from childhood, Ruth Schapiro (Chapter 6), the daughter of the cantor in the town where she came from in Bavaria and a resident of the same apartment building she once lived in. Many years later, my mother told me that she had exchanged locks of hair with her friend the night she left Germany for America as a sign of eternal friendship. Unfortunately, her friend had no way out of Germany and was murdered a few years later at Auschwitz.

Ever since discovering that curl of hair in my grandmother's dining room buffet, I have been of the opinion that the best way to teach children about the Holocaust is through personal contact with survivors and witnesses to the greatest crime in the annals of history. In that spirit, I sought to document the experiences of Holocaust survivors who live "in our midst" in New York's Southern Tier where I now live and present their words, lives and pictures to the children of our area. More than anyone else, our neighbors, friends and families can teach us about what happened to the Jewish people during Hitler's reign of terror in Europe. This book is by no means comprehensive. It is only a partial report, an attempt to find a lock of hair or a memoir or a picture which will connect new generations to events which should never, ever be forgotten.

In Our Midst is organized chronologically. Each selection attempts to illustrate a major theme in Holocaust history. Beginning with pre-war Jewish life in Europe, this anthology includes such topics as Kristallnacht, the voyage of the St. Louis, the battle for the Warsaw Ghetto, hidden children, life and death at Auschwitz and the liberation of Dachau to mention a few. All the reports were made by either individuals living in the Southern Tier or relatives who have settled elsewhere. However, every chapter, every document has a local connection. The Holocaust was not a distant event. It has impacted all our lives. For some of us and our neighbors, it remains the experience which shaped and defined us.

The range of materials used in this collection is broad. Original documents, memoirs and local newspaper accounts from the 1930s and 1940s were secured early in this project. Also, a sustained effort was made to conduct and record oral interviews with area survivors. Second generation reports are included as well in *In Our Midst,* to demonstrate the enduring legacy of the Holocaust.

To make the material accessible to students beginning at the middle school level, some passages have been rewritten or condensed by various editors and researchers who worked with me in this project. When possible, edited materials were returned to the original informants for verification of chronology, fact and mood. Difficult decisions had to be made about including the more graphic material particularly photographs that we secured. On the other hand, some images are simply too horrible to share in a school setting. We hope that our choices were judicious, that everything in this book is usable by teachers in their classrooms and that some of the horror of the Holocaust is reflected in its pages.

A number of people have helped in the creation of *In Our Midst*. First and foremost, I want to thank the survivors and witnesses who agreed to be interviewed and gave us their documents and pictures. Without their cooperation, which involved painful encounters with unpleasant memories to say the least, this book would never have appeared. Second, my warm, personal thanks to my assistant editor, Mary Rose, who also served as the librarian of Temple Concord. Her dedication to this project has been inspiring.

Many people from the Binghamton area, mostly volunteers, were involved in creating this book. A special word of thanks is also due to our staff: Stephanie Horowitz (cover design), Niti Merhavy (graphic design and layout), Tamara Owen (proofing), Sharon Steinberg (newspaper and archival research), Jeff Wiesner (editing and writing), Steve Appel (photography), Laura Anechiarico (index), and Peggy Marcus and Gail Schneider (oral interviews). The final aspects of producing and publishing *In Our Midst* were expertly handled by Professor Parviz Morewedge and his wonderful staff at Binghamton University. The advice and personal support of Dr. Steven Luckert, formerly of Binghamton, N.Y., and now Permanent Exhibition Coordinator of the United States Holocaust Memorial Museum (Washington, D.C.), was invaluable.

The publication of this book was made possible by a generous gift from the Temple Concord Foundation, Earl Gordon, president. The Foundation as well as the congregation of Temple Concord have always been highly supportive of my research and academic work. An additional grant was given by the Susan Matties Nadel Fund of Temple Concord. Special thanks to Bruce Becker for helping obtain materials for Chapter 11 and Doris

Zolty (see Chapter 13) for her support and patience. Barry Rothfeld, editor of the *Press & Sun-Bulletin* and Marc Goldberg, editor of *The Reporter,* the weekly paper of the Jewish Federation of Broome County, both graciously allowed us to reprint materials from their newspapers. Without the local financial support of individuals too numerous to mention, *In Our Midst* would never have been brought to completion.

Dr. Ed Goldenberg, a survivor of six camps and a well known lecturer on the Holocaust, whose experiences are reflected in the pages of this book (Chapter 15), often tells his audiences in the Southern Tier that his biggest fear about the Holocaust is that the enormity of its crimes will be lost to future generations and "It will become a footnote in history." I hope that *In Our Midst* will help preserve a vital link in our area between the generation that experienced the wrath of Nazi hatred and the new generation, which will grow to maturity in the twenty-first century. Together we must keep the flame of memory and hope alive.

Rabbi Lance J. Sussman, Ph.D.

Editor

The Nazis used mass gatherings to stir passions and win support. Source: Nazi Rally pictures 1934-35.

Source: Nazi Rally pictures 1934-35.

Ghettos and Concentration Camps

———	Boundary of Poland until 1939
- - - -	German-Russian Border, 1939–1941
⋙	Concentration Camps
■	Ghettos

CHAPTER 1

A Brief History of the Holocaust

Throughout history, there have been many horrible events and massacres. Countless numbers of innocent people have been victimized by marauding hordes, undisciplined troops, soldiers acting on direct orders from their commanders, and even entire armies following directives from high political authorities. Unfortunately, genocide, the attempt of one group of people to completely eliminate another group of people, is an all too familiar theme in humanity's long, bloody history.

Among these many horrible events the Holocaust of the Jews of Europe from 1933 to 1945 is unique. For twelve years, the government of Nazi Germany dedicated the total resources of a modern, industrial state to the annihilation of the Jewish people. In their zeal, the Nazis employed technological and industrial strategies to eliminate the Jewish people. Their actions were driven by a deep racial hatred of the Jews and fortified by a pseudoscientific theory which maintained that, unless they were totally exterminated, the Jews through intermarriage would prevent the Germans from becoming the master Aryan race of the world. By the end of World War II, although the Nazis murdered six million Jews, they did not succeed in their goal of the total annihilation of the Jewish people.

The roots of Nazi anti-Semitism are long and complex. In part, they derived from the simple tension which exists between people of different backgrounds who live in close proximity to one another. They were also reinforced by hostile religious views, which held Jews collectively responsible for the death of Jesus.

Beginning with the First Crusade at the end of the 11th century, violence against the Jews of Germany became a regular, sad feature of central European history. In 1215, the Fourth Lateran Council determined that Jews were required to dress differently than Christians and, among other things, wear a special Jewish badge. A little more than 300 years later Martin Luther, the great leader of the Protestant Reformation, viciously attacked the Jews of Germany because of their refusal to convert to his branch of Christianity. Today, most churches have fully renounced religious anti-Semitism and seek cordial relations with their Jewish neighbors.

Anti-Semitism in German culture, however, became a permanent feature. It even appeared in German folk tales, in which Jews were often depicted as unscrupulous business people and enemies of the German people. For instance, in a story called "The Jew Among the Thorns," the widely read Grimm brothers offer a tale about a traveling Jew who was brutally tortured for suspicion of petty economic crimes.

At one point in the story, the Jewish victim is forced to dance in a sticker bush. His accuser had a magic fiddle obtained from a dwarf that, when played, compelled all who heard it to dance. As the Jew danced among the thorns, sustaining numerous cuts and injuries, his tormentor cried out, "You have fleeced people often enough, now the thorn bushes shall do the same to you."

During the 18th century, in the time of the Enlightenment, a number of German intellectuals rejected the old, negative stereotypes of the Jews. Instead, they argued that Jews are like everyone else and should be accepted as full members of society. Others insisted that Jews were not Germans and could never become Germans, at least not without converting to Christianity. For a brief period following Napoleon's conquest of Germany, Jews enjoyed increased political rights. Many of the gains, however, were reversed after the French were defeated in 1815. The debate over the political rights of Jews, in Germany as well as in several other European states and collectively referred to as "The Jewish Question," continued to rage throughout much of the 1800s.

The slow, uneven progress of German-Jewish emancipation was offset by the remarkable cultural achievements of the German-Jewish community. As the doors of opportunity opened, Jews began to distinguish themselves in art, literature, science, sports and business. Formerly viewed as "Jews in Germany," they now understood themselves as "German Jews," proud bearers of two cultural traditions. However, not everyone in Germany was happy about the progress of Jewish cultural integration.

By the time Adolf Hitler was born in Braunau, Austria, in 1889, new, well organized anti-Semitic political parties had gained a foothold in German politics as well as in the Reichstag, the German Parliament. Blaming the Jews for the rise of world communism, Germany's defeat in World War I, and its postwar economic problems, Hitler emerged as a leader of German anti-Semitism in the interwar period. In his lengthy, rambling 1925 book, *Mein Kampf* (My Struggle), written in jail after an unsuccessful coup attempt, he spelled out his fascist philosophy and hinted at plans to exterminate the Jewish people.

At first, few people understood the real potential of Nazism giving

Hitler the opportunity to build a massive political party. In 1933, following an impressive showing of his Nazi party in national elections, Hitler was named Chancellor of Germany. Still lacking a clear political majority, he moved quickly to eliminate all political opposition and started stripping Jews of all their political rights and economic opportunities. Nazi thugs harassed Jews in the streets of Germany. Jewish books were burned at Nazi rallies. Jewish places of business were boycotted and picketed by Nazi activists wearing their uniforms of brown shirts, boots, and arm bands with swastikas. By the thousands, German Jews began seeking asylum in foreign lands only to be rebuffed by immigration quotas, anti-Semitism abroad, and international indifference.

On September 15, 1935, the situation worsened for Germany's Jews with the passage of the Nuremberg Racial Laws. Three years later a violent, nationwide pogrom, remembered as Kristallnacht (November 9-10, 1938), named after the tens of thousands of broken windows, resulted in the destruction of nearly all of Germany's synagogues and signaled a major escalation in Hitler's anti-Jewish policies. Concentration camps, already developed by the Nazis, quickly filled with Jewish and political prisoners. By September 1, 1939, when the Nazis launched their blitzkrieg attack on Poland, approximately 60 percent of Germany's 600,000 Jews had fled the country. The remaining 200,000 German Jews, like the rest of Europe's Jewish population, were trapped without an avenue of escape.

Poland, unlike Germany, had a massive Jewish population of over three million people. To control the situation, the conquering Nazis systematically began quarantining the Jewish population there. Jews were forced out of their homes and villages into crowded, unsanitary ghettos, particularly in the larger cities of Warsaw, Krakow and Lodz.

Death rates soared as hunger, disease and Nazi cruelty increased.

On June 22, 1941, Hitler betrayed Stalin, breaking his nonaggression treaty with the Soviet Union. The German army began pushing east to the gates of Stalingrad. At its height, the Nazi empire extended from the northern coast of Norway to the southern tip of Greece and from Normandy in the west to the banks of the Don and Volga Rivers in the USSR. The dark shadow of Nazism had now fallen over most of Europe.

On its eastern front, the Nazis encountered yet another large Jewish civilian population. Impatient with their progress in Poland, the Nazi high command dispatched special SS units called Einsatzgruppen to liquidate the Jewish population in Russia. In the course of just two days, September 29 and 30, 1941, at a ravine called Babi Yar near the Ukrainian city of Kiev, the SS machine gunned 34,000 Jews to death. Similar mass executions took place in the northern sector, near the cities of Kovno and Vilna.

Plans for the "Final Solution" of the Jewish people were drawn up at the Wannsee Conference near Berlin on January 20, 1942. Hitler and his lieutenants envisioned the mass execution of 11 million Jews. Adopting an industrial model, the Nazi commanders began developing the idea of huge death camps with large gas chambers and crematoria. The Auschwitz concentration camp in southern Poland, which opened on April 27, 1940, was now expanded into an extermination industrial complex. By the time of its liberation, a million Jews were murdered at Auschwitz its ovens fed by a train system which operated day and night, in all weather and military conditions. Other death factories were built at Chelmno, Sobibor, Treblinka and Madjdanek. Orders went out to liquidate the ghettos, and eventually plans were made to eliminate the Jews of West Europe in the ovens of the great death camps.

With the Russian victory at Stalingrad early in February 1943, the tide began changing in favor of the allies. As the Nazis were slowly pushed back on all fronts, they continued to wage their genocidal campaign against the Jewish people, often at the expense of their war efforts against the Americans, British, French, and Soviets. Rescue operations to save the remaining Jews of Europe were limited, even though the Allies were aware of the scope and intensity of the Final Solution. Rescue by civilians was a complicated, risky business. Only a relatively few individuals endangered their lives to protect Jews from their Nazi persecutors.

Jewish resistance to Nazism during the Holocaust is hard to assess. Few people believed or predicted that Hitler actually meant to kill all the Jews of Europe. Germany, after all, was a civilized country, a leader in culture and science. For their part, German Jews were quickly and systematically stripped of their rights and livelihoods. Further to the East, the Nazi war machine had an organized plan to round up, control, and eventually dispose of the Jewish population. The Jews, needless to say, were civilians and had no weapons. Hundreds of thousands went to their death as an act of religious martyrdom. Some, like Anne Frank, kept diaries, wrote poetry or drew pictures as forms of moral resistance.

Active, military Jewish resistance also developed during the war. On April 19, 1943, the Jews of the Warsaw Ghetto rose in rebellion against the Nazis. Their heroic example sparked similar rebellions in other ghettos. Jews also created their own partisan units and, in some cases, joined national partisan operations like the French Marquis. In the various Allied armies, particularly the Soviet forces, Jews served with distinction and valor.

The war in Europe ended with V-E Day on May 8, 1945. The fighting in the Pacific continued throughout the summer. As many as 25,000,000 people died in World War II. Entire countries lay ruined. Among the dead were six million Jewish civilians, including 1.5 million Jewish children victims of a racial war conducted by the Nazis with unrelenting savagery. Europe, the principal area of Jewish settlement and the leading site of Jewish cultural and religious activity in the world for centuries, was now almost devoid of synagogues and Jewish schools. Entire families had perished leaving no descendants. Villages had simply disappeared after generations.

Displaced Persons camps were set up for the survivors of the Holocaust. Few wanted to remain in Europe; most wanted to relocate in British Palestine, a distant dream until the State of Israel was established in May 1948. Meanwhile, leading Nazi war criminals were rounded up and tried, beginning with the Nuremberg trials on November 20, 1945. Some are still at large today. A de-Nazification program was also established and, at least in West Germany, the German people agreed to pay reparations. Slowly, the Jewish people began to heal and rebuild.

As the twentieth century draws to a close, the number of Holocaust survivors is diminishing rapidly. Great efforts have been made to record their stories for legal and historical purposes. Museums, memorials, and research institutes have been established, principally in the United States and Israel.

Unfortunately, a revisionist movement has also sprung up which denies that the Holocaust ever took place or else asserts it was dramatically smaller than what even Nazi records suggest. Revisionists' lies have penetrated college campuses and infiltrated the minds of young people everywhere. The motives of the revisionists are vicious; their claims of historical accuracy are, at best, absurd.

This book seeks to help preserve a small part of the history of the Holocaust, by concentrating on the experiences of residents of New York's Southern Tier and their relatives who directly experienced the Nazi war against the Jews of Europe. It does not seek to tell the whole story. However, it does aim to convey a sense of the scope of the tragedy of European jewry through depicting the lives and experiences of people who are our neighbors, friends, and family members, as well as to add, in some small measure, to our overall knowledge of the Holocaust.

This is a book about your neighbors. It is not about distant events and unconfirmed reports. It is about people who live in your town, your county, your state. Read their words carefully. Look at their pictures. Examine their documents. Remember the six million members of their extended family, people just like them, just like you, who did not survive.

Never forget them.

Never.

CHAPTER 2

Jewish Life in Germany Before the War

Norbert Adler fled Germany in 1938, a year before Hitler's inva-sion of Poland began World War II, and three months before Kri-stallnacht, "The Night of Shattered Glass," when Hitler's murderous intentions against the Jews became clear, Adler, then 25, escaped first to Cuba, and then to the United States, where he arranged for his parents to join him from Berlin. During the war, he worked as a draftsman at Ansco, in Binghamton, and since then has run printing and public relations firms.

Adler's family, like other German Jews in the early 1930s, be-lieved at first that Hitler's madness would not engulf them. Many members of his extended family died in the concentration camps.

"Our family had lived in Germany for hundreds of years and a certain amount of ill-placed pride had developed in being German. We weren't like the Jews who came from the ghetto and were segre-gated. We were full-fledged emancipated Germans and very proud of it. My father was a merchant. He ran a leather goods store. He was never a successful businessman and never made a lot of money. Even-tually he sold advertising novelties.

"You have to realize, it didn't start with murder. It started with political rallies. It started with fights between communists and Nazis and socialists and liberals and so on. We were surrounded by it but, if you were not a political person, you could feel that you were not af-fected.

Despite significant anti-Semitism, German Jews felt at home in Germany before 1933. Pictures are from the Erwin Lesser family album (Hamburg, Germany) in the possession of Rabbi Sussman.

"You didn't know the truth from the rumors. You couldn't tell them apart. Was something you heard true or not? And the things you heard were sometimes so unbelievable. We would rationalize, deny what was happening. We would say, 'This couldn't possibly happen: or it didn't happen to me: or it's only this one case.' As we know, what happened afterwards was even more unbelievable.

"We heard stories of people who were being retrained, of people being put in 'retraining camps,' which was the early name of the concentration camps. But I would say, 'Well, I'm not political. I'm clean. They won't bother me.'"

"I know that my aunts, uncles and cousins all died in the concentration camps. There is a story in my family that talks about my grandmother's deportation. And the hearsay is that she jumped off the train, rather than be taken to the concentration camps.

"Last year, my kids and I went to Israel and we did some research. They have books there that list the names of people killed in the Holocaust. We saw her name, and it said 'Auschwitz; and a question mark after it. There was also a German word, Verschollen, which means 'disappeared without trace.' And that term was used with my grandmother's name. I still carry the notion that she jumped off that train. And that was her last act of courage.'"

Source: *Binghamton Press and Sun-Bulletin,* December 4, 1991.

CHAPTER 3

Jewish Life in Poland Before the War

James B. Gitlitz is a retired Binghamton attorney and a well-known amateur photographer. In 1937, he traveled throughout Central and Eastern Europe. Although his pictures of his trip through the "heartland" of Jewish Europe were lost many years ago, this report of pre-Holocaust Jewish life in Poland survived.

The Polish Jew, unlike his German brother, has never become assimilated. In the ghettos of Warsaw and Lwow (formerly Lemberg), where the accompanying pictures were taken, you can see him today a dirty, unkempt figure, with a long beard and earlocks, large hat and long black coat, striding along the crowded walks or in the street itself, or arguing on any street corner. Desperately he clings to his alien dress, associating in his mind ancient manners and customs with the ritual of his religion.

There are other Jews in Poland, it is true. In the coffee shops of Warsaw and Lemberg, and in the night clubs, in the Cafe Esplanade and the Cafe Adria, you will see young Jewish men and women as smartly dressed as in the New Yorker and the Rainbow Room. But they are the exception: they have, in some fortuitous way, solved their individual problem, at least for the time being.

The Pole still looks upon this stranger in his midst with suspicion and distrust. He begrudges the stranger a living when he must struggle so hard himself. He has lived with him all his life (the Jew comprises almost ten percent of the population of Poland), but he has never come to know him.

In Vilno, my companion saw a doroszka driver slash a Jew across the face with his whip so violently that blood followed. A Polish policeman looked on, unconcerned. In the same town, he saw a Jewish woman and her two children living in a packing box. In Lwow a Jewish shopkeeper, who ran a tiny business selling tea and cakes, was unable to pay the arbitrary figure assessed him by the tax collector. They sent his boy home from school as the tax collectors took his mirrors from the walls of his shop. "In some cases:" he complained to me bitterly, "they back a wagon up to a shop and dismantle it."

"What are we going to do," he asked me sadly, and I gave him the only possible and characteristically Jewish reply. I shrugged my shoulders.

Poland owes its present independence almost entirely to the efforts of the United States at the close of the World War. Created by the

Jewish Community leaders of Kletzk, White Russia, 1922
Source: *Kletzk Journal, 1946*

Versailles treaty, Poland guaranteed to preserve equal rights for all minorities within its borders. The death of Pilsudski, however, marked the beginning of an open revolt against the limitations of the Versailles treaty. In this respect, as in others, the actions of its western neighbor served as a handy model.

Under Marshal Rydz-Smigly, the real ruler of Poland, and with the open and official approval of President Moscicki, there has been organized the "Camp of National Unity." Its slogan is "Poland for the Poles" and its aim the authoritarian state. From its membership all minority peoples are excluded Ukrainians, Germans, Lithuanians, Ruthenians and Czechs, as well as Jews, altogether comprising about one-third of the population of Poland. But with the Slavic minorities the government's policy is one of non-equality and compromise; with the Jew it is frankly one of ouster.

The New York Times of June 4, 1937, states: "According to one government spokesman, it is its desire that at least 50,000 Jews should emigrate monthly, preferably youths."

To accomplish its purpose the government has resorted to ancient and well-tried methods: propaganda of race libel, economic strictures, educational bars, and even open violence. From February 1 to June 30, 1937, an incomplete report shows 152 attacks on Jews in different places in Poland, with 426 Jews injured and 22 killed. When I was in Warsaw in April of this year, the University had been closed because of open rioting between Polish and Jewish students. Two major pogroms occurred within five weeks in May and June, at Brest-Litovsk and at Czestochowa, without police interference.

Source: *Jewish Center Yearbook,* Binghamton, NY, 1937.

4

Emigration Prior to the War

Leaving Europe was always very traumatic. Germaine Rosenberg and Meta Mendel, two Binghamton residents, tell of their flight from Germany and their resettlement on farms near Binghamton. The German Jews who settled in the Binghamton area during the 1930s-1940s founded the "Get Together" club to offer one another support and friendship.

Germaine Rosenberg

I was born November 14, 1914, in Langenthal, Switzerland. My father was Henry Vischoff and my mother was Berta Katz Vischoff. My father, who was in the textile business, came from Russia, moved to Switzerland, and was well educated. My mother was from France and attended Hebrew school. I had no formal religious training and couldn't read Hebrew. I was the only Jewish child in the town because my sister was 16 years older. I attended junior college in Berne and Yaronne business school.

In 1932, additional Jewish children were in the area. My husband-to-be, Fritz Rosenberg, arrived from Germany. His father died when Fritz was 13, and his mother supported them as a milliner. Fritz came to Switzerland by himself and, in 1934, went to agricultural college there. He and I met at Passover and were married in 1937. As Switzerland was anti-Jewish and anti-German, we considered leaving the country. Fritz wanted to go to Germany, but I preferred to come to the U.S. In April of 1939, we took the *USS Washington* from Le Havre to the U.S. Since we sailed in tourist class, we did not have to go to Ellis Island.

When I married Fritz, I lost my Swiss citizenship; a wife had to revert to the citizenship of her husband. That is why my passport has a "J" stamped on it, and the German swastika.

Meta Mendel

I was born in Weiler, Germany, on December 14,1908.1 had one brother, who was older than me, and my family's name was Anspach.

Weiler was a small, resort town, in the Rhineland area of Germany. My father was in the cattle business. There were few local Jewish families. My parents kept a kosher home, but there was no temple nearby. The temple was in another small town, where we went for Yom Tov. My father was the cantor and blew the shofar on Rosh Hashanah.

I went to school in Sobercheim, at a gymnasium. It was a private school; I received religious instruction in town after school. When I completed the gymnasium, I took cooking and sewing lessons. In 1932, I got married in Germany to Sigmund Mendel. He was from Niederwiesen, and his family was also in the cattle business. He was five years older than I.

My father was in WWI, as a cook in a hospital unit. I remember visiting him there during the war. After the war, French soldiers occupied homes in Germany. During the time I went to the gymnasium, I couldn't take the train, as the French soldiers took the train. All children had to ride bicycles to school, so during the winter I stayed at the gymnasium.

When Hitler came into power in 1933, there was not much campaigning for him in our small town. People who supported him would come into the town. Sigmund and I stayed engaged for 13 months, thinking that Hitler would fall.

One day, my husband and brother-in-law went to a farm in a car. When they arrived, the farmer said that the Germans were looking for them. They escaped through a sewer system and got a ride on a log wagon back home. Later, at night, they went back to get the car.

My son Eric was born in 1934. I used to have a young German girl as a helper with Eric, but she had to stop working for me. A teacher of hers said, "If anybody sees you with that little Jew, you can't come back to school." This event made us think of leaving during the years of 1935-36. We looked into Israel, but an aunt had already obtained affidavits for 92 relatives to emigrate there.

Our cleaning lady also told us that she couldn't work for us anymore because we were Jews. She couldn't afford to face the consequences of working for Jews.

When we left, we were able to take some of our possessions but were allowed to take no money. My husband, Sigmund, worked to get some of the money out through his relatives who lived in Luxembourg. On the day we were able to leave, we stopped first in Luxembourg to get the money from a bank there. We then found our way to a ship and came to America in steerage, because of health problems that kept us from a higher class of travel. We came into Ellis Island.

Source: Conversations with Germaine Rosenberg and Meta Mendel, Binghamton, NY, 1991.

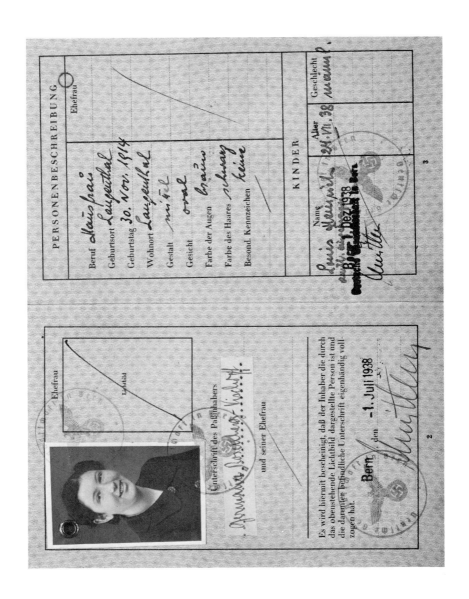

Germaine Rosenberg's "Racial" Passport, 1938

CHAPTER 5

Dr. Fritz Loewenstein

The most widely read eyewitness account of the Holocaust was written by a young Jewish girl in hiding in Amsterdam, In her diary, Anne Frank writes about Peter Von Pels, who was in hiding with her. The following story by Fritz Loewenstein, a medical doctor in Binghamton, describes Peter and his family prior to their emigration to Holland.

Dr. Fritz Loewenstein was 10 years old when he left Osnabruck, Germany, with his family. But as a Jew, he had already experienced countless acts of prejudice and had witnessed Nazi attacks on other Semites.

"I felt a good deal of discrimination," said Loewenstein, 68, who lives in Binghamton. "I could not possibly have gone to public schools because I would have been beaten constantly. Friends who were not Jewish, after a time, were instructed by their parents not to play with me.

"I felt as a boy, 'What is wrong with me? Why is it that people mistreat me?'

"Conditions became worse, year by year. It was like an ever-tightening noose. There were beatings in the street. There was increasing pressure on the (German) people not to use Jewish stores. Life became increasingly difficult and tenuous for Jewish families in Germany, so that people with foresight began to make plans to leave the country."

He described members of paramilitary groups, dressed in brown uniforms with swastikas on their arm bands, who patrolled the street of Osnabruck. "It was utter brutality," Loewenstein said. "Storm troopers, people in brown uniforms, young thugs, would surround a Jew and beat him senseless. This was an everyday occurrence."

Jews eventually were banned from public schools, and he and his sister had to attend a one-room school in the synagogue. About 20 students grades 1-8 filled the room, including a boy who became known to the world through the diary of Anne Frank, Peter Von Pels. "I don't think he was a happy boy," Loewenstein said, "He was shy and retiring."

In 1936, the Von Pels family emigrated to the Netherlands, where Peter's father joined Anne Frank's father, Otto, in a spice business. In 1942, the families went into hiding together, when the Nazis began to take Jews from Amsterdam. The families were discovered August 4, 1944. Peter Von Pels died in the death camp Mauthausen in 1945. Loewenstein's father left Germany in 1936, to establish himself in the United States. The rest of the family followed the next year.

Source: *Binghamton Press & Sun-Bulletin,* April 26,1995.

CHAPTER 6

Kristallnacht

Beginning on the night of November 8, 1938, the Nazi government of Germany organized a massive campaign of violence against the Jews and Jewish property throughout the Reich. During the following 24 hours, nearly every synagogue in Germany was destroyed and tens of thousands of Jewish businesses were wrecked. Because of all the broken glass scattered on sidewalks and streets, the campaign became known as Kristallnacht. The following account of Kristallnacht is a condensed version of a talk given by Rabbi Sussman on the fiftieth anniversary of the Night of Broken Glass.

My family, on my mother's side, lived in Germany during the time of Kristallnacht (the night of broken glass). I am now an adult, yet I only recently heard about their experience. My mother rarely talks about her childhood in Germany. The subject comes up only in passing. The fear, the constant threat of violence, and the sickening feeling of having to leave her family behind are all memories she prefers to leave undisturbed.

When Hitler came to power in 1933, my mother was eight years old. Her home was in Bamberg, Germany. It was an ancient town surrounded by mountains. Jewish people resided here for over a thousand years. My grandparents owned a company that manufactured thread and thread products and, like many German Jews of that time, they prospered. However, my mother knew the lack of privileges that came with being a Jew. She shrugs her shoulders even today, in protest that she "simply didn't understand." She couldn't go certain places because she was a Jew; adults whispered things that had to do with being Jewish; and her uncles Heiner and Siegbert left the country. For an eight-year-old, these things didn't add up. For most adults it didn't add up.

In the fall of 1935, the Nuremberg racial laws went into effect which, among other things, forbade all Jewish children from attending public schools. My mother and her friends would have to go to the afternoon Hebrew School for the full day. Eighty to a hundred children from Bamberg and the surrounding areas crowded into the school. The shades were drawn, there were no playground activities, and more and more teachers were taken by the Nazis, until only two remained.

My mother began to see Nazism everywhere. Nazi storm troopers paraded the streets of Bamberg, brandishing flags with swastikas. There was no escape from the Nazi presence at home, either. The shutters were usually kept closed and, if the Nazis came, my mother and her brother were assigned a hiding place under a large desk. The desk became a place to retreat to when danger threatened.

The synagogue became the last place that the Jews of Bamberg felt free. My mother joined the choir and has wonderful memories of the synagogue. She said once of her time there, "you weren't afraid to be Jewish when you sang."

But everyday life was different. In 1937, a group of Nazi soldiers threatened to rape and drown my mother and two of her friends. The three girls had gone on a bike ride, stopping at a lake in the hills to rest. When the Nazis appeared and made their threats, the three friends fled and were chased back to the city by the Nazis. In the wake of this incident, my grandparents for the first time considered getting their daughter out of the country. A short time later, the kosher butcher's son disappeared. One day he vanished, and no one was ever able to find out what happened to him. My grandparents made their decision. It was impossible for the whole family to leave Germany together, and my uncle was too young to go alone. The decision was that my mother would leave for the United States by herself with the hope that the rest of the family would follow later.

After dark, parents and daughter wound thread around money hidden in spools to smuggle out of the country with my mother for her passage to freedom. On the evening before she left, friends came to say good-bye, many of whom were also trying to leave. One in particular, Ruth Schapiro, remains vivid in my mother's mind. Ruth did not have a sponsor a relative or friend to receive her in another country. She and my mother said good-bye and each cut off a curl of hair to give to the other for a remembrance. Ruth never found a sponsor and was murdered in a concentration camp. Her curl is still in my family's possession.

The next morning my mother left Bamberg and began a voyage which brought her to relatives in New York. She was now free, but the rest of the family was still in Germany.

Conditions in Germany became much worse. Many Jews, my grandparents included, were forced by the Nazis to sell their businesses at a fraction of their worth. Other Jewish businesses were shut down. All Jews' identification papers had to be stamped with a "J." Violence increased. Hitler Youth beat my uncle. My mother's uncle was arrested and sent to the concentration camp Dachau, and executed for going to the bathroom without permission.

On November 7, 1938, Nazi ambassador Ernest Vom Rath was assassinated in Paris. Herschel Grynszpan, a German Jewish 17-year-old, shot Vom Rath in retaliation for the Nazis' October deportation of his parents to Poland. The Nazis used Vom Rath's death as an excuse to unleash an organized effort of violence against Germany's Jews. Jews were to be rounded up en masse. Kristallnacht had arrived.

By early morning of November 9, 1938, violence and destruction surrounded every German Jew. In the next 24 hours, 1118 synagogues and 7500 Jewish-owned businesses throughout Germany were vandalized or completely destroyed. A thousand Jews were murdered, and 30,000 more were sent to concentration camps.

Shortly after midnight on November 10, the Nazis came to Bamberg. They met at the Messerschmidt Restaurant. From there, they marched the short distance to my mother's synagogue. On the outside of the synagogue they painted anti-Semitic graffiti; every door read "OUT

JEW." Nazis soaked the inside of the synagogue with gasoline and set it ablaze. Bamberg's last bastion of Jewish freedom was in flames. Willy Lessing, a leading Jewish citizen, rushed to save the Torahs, or holy scrolls. The Nazis attacked and beat him with metal bars. Later that night, the Nazis appeared at the Lessing home. Unsatisfied that Mr. Lessing had survived, the Nazis pulled him from his bed and savagely attacked him again. It took the intervention of Bamberg's archbishop to have Mr. Lessing admitted to a hospital. Willy Lessing died eight weeks later from his wounds. At dawn, the Nazis took my grandfather. Horrified, my grandmother asked her former laundress, an elderly non-Jewish woman named Berta, to go to the city jail and explain to the officials that her husband had permission to leave Germany. Berta

Bamberg Jewish School-Elementary Grades 1936-1937

"To my left, girl with braids is Ruth Schapiro whose lock of hair I have. She was deported and died in Auschwitz as did her father, Cantor Schapiro 3rd row, second from left. Other two teachers survived. Mr. Frankl (right) went to Cincinnati and Mr. Fleishman was last heard of in NYC.
Majority of kids shown did not 'make it.'"

Quote by Freda Sacki Sussman.

not only went to the jail but arranged for my grandfather's release. There were many people like Berta, non-Jews, who did not succumb to the evil and inhumanity that was Nazism. People like Berta saved lives.

My grandfather returned home, and the family left by train for Holland. They only stayed a short time, then boarded a ship for Hoboken, NJ, where they arrived on December 15, 1938, to rebuild their lives.

Source: Sermon,
Rabbi Sussman, 1988.

*At left, Frieda Sacki,
Bamberg, c. 1930*

*At bottom, Kurt and Frieda Sacki,
Bamberg, 1937.*

CHAPTER 7

St. Louis

Hitler's aggressive measures against the Jews of Germany led to a sharp rise in immigration during the late 1930s. One of the most famous incidents involved the inability of a ship, the S.S. St. Louis, to find a safe port for the refugees it was carrying. After crossing the Atlantic, its passengers were refused entry in numerous places, and the St. Louis was forced to return most of those on board to Germany. The following letter was in the possession of Abraham Fink's grandfather of Jean Hecht, former president of Binghamton's Temple Concord. Fink was active with the American Joint Distribution Committee. The letter refers to the JDC's attempt to persuade the Cuban government to allow the refugees on the St. Louis into its country.

"In reply to your cable, regarding refugees on board the *SS St. Louis,* you know, dear Mr. Rosenberg, that Cuba has contributed, in relation to its resources and population, to a greater extent than any other nation, in order to give hospitality to persecuted people. But it is completely impossible to accede to this immigrant entry into national territory. The subject of St. Louis is completely closed by the government. I regretfully reiterate the impossibility of their entry into Cuba. I wish to assure you of my sincere friendship.

Laredo Bru."

Source: Typescript, June 15, 1939,
American Joint Distribution Committee.

CHAPTER 8

Escape from Paris

Every Jew who escaped from Europe has a story to tell. Sam Goldin, who was born in Poland and educated in France, narrowly escaped from the Nazi army. He later settled in Binghamton, NY, and was successful in the food canning industry.

I was born in Poland on May 1, 1916. The city has since become Nieswieze, Russia. My father, Moshe, owned a lumber mill. He came from a family of lumber business owners. He had two brothers. One died an early death, killed by the Bolsheviks in the Russian Revolution of 1917. The other died of a heart attack. My mother had six siblings. Two remained in Europe. I have two sisters who live in New York City. One is a dentist and the other is an administrator of a Methodist church.

In 1926, my family and I moved to Warsaw, Poland, because my father wished to build a plant for his lumber mill there. From 1926-1937, I attended a private school. I took Hebrew and Jewish courses taught in a Zionist, rather than a religious, vein. I wanted to attend a university in Poland, so I took the required Baccalaureate exam. I was denied entrance because of Jewish quotas. In 1937, I went to France after my graduation from high school, since I would be unable to attend school in Poland. In France, I enrolled as a chemical engineering student at the University of Strasbourg.

Two years later, problems caused by the war became apparent in France. Contact with my family in Warsaw was impossible, so I was no longer able to receive money from them. My sister came to France to visit. She was without a visa, but managed to avoid deportation by staying with a Polish-Jewish family in France.

My financial problems eased temporarily when I befriended a Jewish family from Poland. They fed me until I was able to find a job working on a farm. Farm workers were in demand since most French men had joined the military. I considered joining the Foreign Legion, but decided against it when my university allowed me to continue studying for free. I found a job as an extra in the theater, and eventually became a stagehand. These jobs enabled me to rent an apartment for my sister and myself until 1940. Hitler would soon push through France and we would have to flee.

Upon hearing explosions and gun fire in the distance, people began to move south. The University of Strasbourg campus evacuated to Michelin, France. My sister and I first moved to Bordeaux and soon after had to move farther south to the flat land between Bordeaux and the Pyrenees mountains. A short time later we moved even farther south, because the Germans were close. We went to Marseilles, which was in Free France. I found a job selling pencils with another Jewish student. This earned me enough money to last three weeks.

I wanted to finish my exams at the university. My sister and I went back to Michelin and were able to find an apartment and stay for a while. My other sister, Raya, became waylaid in America as a result of the war. I wrote to her to find out about the possibility of coming to the United States. In 1941, as my sister told me to do, I registered with the American consulate. I obtained a letter from a doctor claiming that I was terminally ill and would die in a few months. This would enable me to attain an exit visa to see my family in America. The scheme worked and several months later I had a permit to leave the country.

After an eighteen-day boat ride, I landed in Brooklyn. When I got off the boat I saw a police officer and became very frightened, but he told me not to worry. My sister eventually got out of France on a

Mexican visa.

All this time we hadn't had contact with my family in Warsaw. I found out that my parents went to the gas chamber immediately upon arriving in Auschwitz my father murdered at the age of 55, and mother at the age of 50.

In 1971, I travelled to Poland. I went to Warsaw and found my father's old factory. I went to Auschwitz. In the many pictures hanging on the walls, I looked for my father's face. It wasn't there.

Source: Conversation with Sam Goldin, 1991

At left, picture of Sam Goldin as a school boy. At right, Sam Goldin with his sister, Raya.

CHAPTER 9

Operation Barbarossa, 1941

Beginning in the late 1880s, a wave of Jewish immigration began streaming from east Europe to the United States. Among the thousands of east European immigrants were a number of Jewish families from the southeast Lithuanian village of Baltermontz. Today, a number of Southern Tier Jewish families can trace their ancestry back to Baltermontz. However, the majority of the Jews of Baltermontz about 200 families remained in Lithuania. All but a few of them perished during the Holocaust.

The following document describes how anti-Semitic elements in the local population took immediate action against the Jews of Butrimantz (=Baltermontz?), once the German army defeated the Soviet military in the Spring of 1941. In the wake of the 1941 Nazi offensive, widely known as Operation Barbarossa, mobile SS units called Einsatzgruppen massacred hundreds of thousands of Jews across the Eastern front.

From June 22, 1941, when the Russians were pushed back by the murderous Germans, it was not long until Butrimantz fell into German hands.

The robbing and murdering of Jews began immediately.

Lithuanian collaborators helped in the attack on the Jews. They drafted the young men for work and also took in the young women who were forced to work under horrible conditions.

They tortured Rabbi Vitkinen. They lit his beard on fire and made him run through the streets of the city with his burning beard. The tormentors cried, "Thus we will do this to all the rabbis." Rabbi Gershon was also tortured.

Other Jews were tortured and shot at while they were working. This did not last too long. At the beginning of September, 1941, a ghetto was established. They took the Jews of the village from a two kilometer radius and from the nearby village of Stokklish and drove them to the two synagogues and murdered them there.

The Chief of Police seized the local doctor and his wife, brought them into the village and locked them in a building. The doors of the building were then cemented shut. The doctor's wife went berserk, but he escaped.

Source: Rabbi Ephraim Oshy, *Hurban Lita* (The Ruins of Lithuania), New York, Montreal, 1951.
Translated from the original Yiddish by Sam Goldin.

10

Fighting in the Warsaw Ghetto

Perhaps the most famous story of Jewish armed resistance during the Holocaust involves the Warsaw Ghetto uprising. The following account, provided by Raya Goldin's friend, Melenka, offers a view from outside the ghetto in April 1943. At the end of the fighting, Melenka writes, "The ghetto was empty and quiet." Raya is Sam Goldin's sister

Henry, my husband, his mother, sister and I found a place to hide. I called it "Melina" which in criminal language means shelter. Our host was a gentile by the name of Dusia, who lived on Muranowska Street. The wall of the ghetto was built along Muranowska Street, dividing the street into Jewish and Aryan sides. It was a dangerous street for hiding since the Germans searched the streets near the Ghetto for Jews trying to escape. Dusia was a member of the Polish underground. In her apartment she had illegal literature and a printing press. Sometimes we heard men coming in and out of the apartment. She was very brave; there was a death penalty for underground activity and for hiding Jews. We had a good room with a window that overlooked the Ghetto.

On the 18th of April, Dusia came into our room. She looked worried. The Germans had replaced all the Polish Gentile policemen who normally guarded parts of the wall. When the Nazis planned something new, they never trusted Polish policeman. Instead they used Ukrainians, or other special units from the Baltic countries, as helpers.

The next morning we heard boots hitting the pavement. We ran to the window and saw German soldiers marching in formation into the Ghetto. Suddenly we heard shooting. The soldiers broke ranks and ran for cover. We heard tanks coming, moving into the Ghetto. Then I noticed two flags on the roof of a tall building in the Ghetto. One was the Jewish blue and white, and the other was the Polish red and white. A child had brought the Polish flag through the sewers. Jewish fighters defended both flags until the end. I promised myself that if I survived, I would tell others about the defiant flags and the people that defended them.

For days there was lots of shooting in the Ghetto, small arms and machine guns. The Nazi gun post was located at the entrance to our building, under the thin wooden floor of Dusia's apartment. Every time the machine gun shot toward the Ghetto, our room shook violently. Suddenly our window shattered. The Jewish fighters had aimed above the machine gun, hitting our window. I felt like a spectator in a gigantic theater. The shooting went on, and the Nazis started burning every house. Smoke filled our room, and the wooden frames of the window blackened. Dusia came to our room and moved us to a back room, as firemen came to pour water on the windows to keep them from catching fire. Dusia told us that as Jews from the ghetto many of them children tried to escape, the Nazis caught and killed them on the Aryan side. After a few days she moved us back to the front room. The ghetto was still burning; there was less and less shooting. We could see Nazis marching groups of people along the street to the square further down. One day, a group of Jews walked, under guard, to where we could see them better. One old woman at the back of the group was slower than the rest. A soldier came close to her and shot her. She fell, leaving a small body on the pavement. At night when I looked out the window again, she seemed to have shrunk. The Jewish guns were nearly silent. The machine guns had stopped long before.

The Germans sent special units into the ghetto. They drilled holes in the walls of all the buildings. Dynamite was put in the holes. There was a deafening noise, and 34 floors of the buildings came down. Once, the Germans brought a young man, a civilian in a leather coat and high boots. They drilled a hole and exploded a wall of the building opposite us. From the ruins, they lead out 15-20 people, mostly women and children, who had probably hidden in a bunker. They marched away under guard. The young man, we thought, was an informer.

Another day, two long, black limousines arrived just opposite us and stopped. A few smartly dressed Nazis, tall, slim and in black or dark uniforms with insignias on them, jumped out. They took photos, then brought a woman from somewhere. They played a game of shooting around her head while she stayed against the wall. She was motionless. She was later taken away.

The ghetto was empty and quiet. Even in June we sometimes heard at night a solitary gun shot, as if someone left in the ghetto wanted to say that the resistance was still alive. Every morning the Ukrainian guards changed. The men sang while marching. They sang a song about a girl, and apple and pear trees in bloom. We liked the song it took us away to another place for a few minutes.

I left the ghetto in 1943. It was my job to stay alive and to be a witness. I have to repeat and repeat what happened to me. It is to be shared with everyone. The more they learn, the more they know, the more they will work to shape the world of happiness for everybody.

Source: Letter to Raya Goldin, 1989.

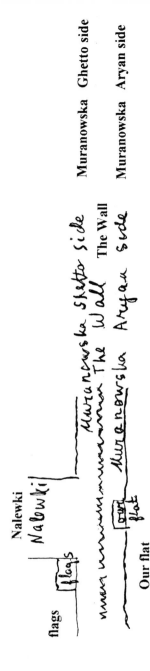

Melinka's hand-drawn map of Warsaw Ghetto, 1985.

CHAPTER 11

I Never Left Janowska

I Never Left Janowska was written by Dr. Helene Kaplan and published after her death. An art historian, Dr. Kaplan was "a hidden child" during the Holocaust. Thousands of Jewish children were saved by non-Jewish families who took responsibility for them. In most instances, they were hidden in cellars and barns. For their own safety they were not allowed to see the outside world. Dr. Kaplan took a greater risk, she posed as a non-Jew in a world that had turned against the Jews.

My Life Before Hiding

I was born in Boryslaw, Poland, a town of 40,000 people, most of whom worked for the oil industry. My father was the Administrative Director of the Polish Oil industry. My immediate family was not religious, but my grandparents were. The family only went to the synagogue on the Jewish New Year and the Day of Atonement. However, the other holidays were celebrated at home with all the family members.

I grew up in a large house with two maids, a cook, coachman, watchman, and a chauffeur. The servants were paid for by the oil company. Father was one of the very few Jewish executives in the Polish oil industry. As a young man, he had been given the task of consolidating all the oil companies into one amalgamated group.

I had one sister, Doneczka. Both of us were educated at home by a governess, and later went to the Gymnasium.

We led a privileged life. We had pet dogs and deer that lived outside in a walled garden. There were many parties at home. Our mother had dresses made for us and we all enjoyed a very social lifestyle. The parties ended when Doneczka died at the age of 19. She was buried in Vienna, Austria. When the family visited the grave during Hitler's occupation of Austria, we noticed a change in the atmosphere. Prior to the occupation, Vienna had been a welcoming place one where the entire family could enjoy the restaurants and activities of a large city. During the occupation, park benches were labeled with signs that read "Juden Verboten" (Jews Forbidden).

On September 1, 1939, I was standing with a few other students from the Gymnasium when a loudspeaker announced that war with Germany had started and that France and England would soon enter it. My father obtained gas masks for the family and started a shelter in the backyard. For a short time we moved from Boryslaw to a place in the countryside, but returned to Boryslaw when we heard of drunken bands of Ukranians looking to kill Jews. Our family did not know what to expect, so we didn't try to leave the country. In mid-September the German Wehrmacht entered the town. The Germans decided to set up their headquarters in our house. There were men stationed outside the house, which now displayed the Nazi flag. At that point in time, the soldiers were very polite. A Russian-German agreement a few weeks later resulted in the Germans leaving and the Russians moving in their tanks and occupying the area.

The Russians (mostly communist sympathizers) were very difficult to deal with. Suddenly, the oil workers were negative towards my father. However, the Russians needed him. They appointed him a general manager of the oil industry in the eastern and western region of what was the Polish Ukraine.

Again our home was occupied, this time by Russians and their families. The Russians seemed very unsure of themselves and refused any assistance or help with western customs. This was a Stalinist period in

Russia, and the people would constantly state that the Russians had invented everything. They carried their guns when they walked from room to room. Even though the family was now restricted to one room, we were still together and able to have fun with each other. There were some deportations to Russia, the first to go were the affluent and the politically prominent people. It was not too hard to avoid Russian deportation, though, since no members of the local population collaborated with the Russians. One could simply hide across the street from your regular home and be spared.

I began school in Lwow, Poland. Before I could be admitted to the university, I had to produce a statement saying that my father worked for the good of the people and did not put down the workers. I was finally admitted into the architecture program. There were many women in the courses, and some chemistry and pharmacy were specifically dominated by women. It was very difficult to befriend the Russian students as they appeared to have a chip on their shoulders. Due to the overcrowding in Lwow, caused by people fleeing the Germans and those introduced by the Russian occupation, everyone was allotted a certain number of square feet. All those who owned apartments were ordered to take on tenants. Once a week, we had to attend an indoctrination lecture presented by the Russian NKVD (the secret police, before the KGB).

Then on June 21, 1941, I heard the distant sound of artillery. Germans were on the move back to Lwow, this time to invade. The Russians fled the area. Local residents prepared for the unknown. For the first few days after the German invasion, there was neither water nor electricity. The next day the square was surrounded by German troops and everyone was directed to show their papers; the Aryans were separated from the Jews. I stood in line with my friend Alma. Neither one of us spoke Yiddish, the common language of some Jews in Europe. However, we did speak fluent German and French. One of the German officers took us out of the line and asked us to work for him in an office. The officer was actually a member of the Austrian Gestapo. He provided us with a very important paper, an "Ausweise;" or work card. Without a card, one could be caught in a roundup and sent away. I was lucky that day. At another spot in Lwow, seven thousand Jews were killed. It was while working for the Austrian Gestapo that I was confronted with the question that often haunted me later in life, "Are you really Jewish? You do not seem different from other girls." I often wondered if I was supposed to be different, just because I happened to be Jewish. Because of the arm bands that we had to wear (the yellow star), we could be pushed around by anyone. As one passed by a soldier, one could be kicked, pushed or thrown in the street. Attacks on Jews seemed to escalate on a daily basis.

The man who employed us was moving to a car repair shop called "Janowska" because it was located on Janowska Street. I was employed in the main reception office. The car shop employed Polish mechanics, whom they paid; other work was done by Jewish workers who were forcibly brought there by the SS and a policemen. As these groups of men and boys were brought in, it was my job to record their names and professions, and assign them to foremen. Some days, the head of the operation, Gebauer, would beat all the men; on others he would be more benevolent.

Eventually I moved closer to Janowska, since there were rumors of a ghetto being formed for the Jews. In mid-October, a large number of Jews were marched into Janowska by the SS. There was not enough food or water for the people. There was no place for the people to sleep, many were outside in the cold and the rain. Wives, mothers and sisters of the men, came to the gate and pleaded to see them or at least give them clothing or food. The SS had the men begin to build barracks Janowska was on its way to becoming a concentration camp. The Gestapo used the names of the men on cards that I had written to ascertain if men were there in the camp or not. If someone did not respond on roll call, others within the camp could be punished. The inmates of the camp looked horrible; they were filthy and bony. The commandant ordered me not to look at them, he said that I was different, and shouldn't associate with them. I was very grateful that no one in my family ever passed through those camp gates.

Hiding

Over the months, I made it back home to visit relatives. Roundups of Jews happened more and more. Anyone who did not look truly Semitic was encouraged to leave the ghetto. Aryan papers could be purchased from Poles or Ukranians provided by friendly priests or nuns, or forged by groups of Jewish chemists. After long talks with my parents, I decided to escape. I bought a passport from the forgers in the name of Krystyna Kozlowska; they also provided me with a false birth certificate. My new nationality was Polish. I had to learn Christian prayers, as the police would ask anyone who was caught to kneel in the street and recite the catechism. From a man who knew my father, I also obtained working papers in my new name, Krystyna Kozlowska.

I set off alone for Lwow. I was initially going to go to Krakow with another person. However, since my papers were not finished yet, the other woman went alone. She unwittingly spoke in Yiddish, instead of the German she thought she spoke, and was killed by the Nazis. I didn't find this out until many years had passed. I made it to Lwow, and found many Poles at the train station who were offering rooms or beds for the night. I followed one man home. He and his wife had fixed up a clean bed in their house, in the same room that they slept in. I lay there listening to the man snore and thought of the new chapter in my life. The next day, I walked the streets of Lwow without my armband. At the post office, I sent a note to my parents through prearranged protocol. While there, I met a blond, Jewish woman I knew. We decided to look for lodging together. We found the perfect spot in the home of a single woman, who let us use an extra bed until her lover, a German Wehrmacht soldier, came to visit; then we would sleep on the kitchen floor. I found a job as a cleaning woman, for the military generals who commanded the prisoners of war camps. My friend, Alma, who was also posing as a Pole, came for a visit. This was very dangerous, but

Alma was one to take risks.

As time went on I became more tense. People in the building where I lived kept asking me why I had come to Lwow. One day, a young Pole approached me and said, "Don't stand here, move quickly. You are being observed, you are Jewish." I yelled back, "Of course not." I was not sure if he was trying to find out or was just suspicious. I was concerned about the woman who helped me with the cleaning. She was always looking at me, and she noticed that I didn't really know how to iron. She helped me fold the clothes, but she kept looking at me. Several days later someone told me that she had been arrested; someone recognized her and denounced her. The woman I was afraid of was Jewish and I didn't know it. I felt so bad all she wanted to do was talk to me.

On a cold day in December, I came back to my room to find my mother there. She had attempted to make herself look Aryan. She wore a bright blouse and earrings and didn't really look Jewish. We kissed and acted casually, as if it were natural for her to visit. Then I found out that the situation at home was worse and my father had arranged for my mother to get new papers. Her new name was Judwiga Kozlowska. My mother stayed for several days. One night while the three of us were asleep, there was a knock at the door, and police were there. They checked my papers; I hid my mother under the covers. I explained to my roommate that my mother didn't have the correct visiting papers yet. The next day my mother left. Through my father's contacts, she arranged to work as a housekeeper for the German director of the oil company.

More and more people were arrested. I began to feel hopeless that I would never be able to survive what lay ahead. When the General who I worked for was away one day, all that worthlessness that I felt welled up. I opened the gas jet in the kitchen and started to inhale. I lost consciousness. I woke up to voices; the General was there. I admitted to him that I was Jewish, and that I did not want to fight for my life any longer. He seemed shocked. I went home feeling more depressed. The next day when I came to work, he told me that he could no longer employ me. He gave me all his food stamps and his best wishes and said that he would not denounce me.

I found another job, at a hospital for the insane. I peeled potatoes and translated for the Italian nurses. Some Italian soldiers from the Russian front would come here for treatment also. But I couldn't work here forever. Two months later I volunteered for a job in Germany. There was nothing else I could do. There was an increase in people going through the area looking for Jews with Aryan papers. One night while I was sitting at the table in my room, the Gestapo came to the door and wanted my papers. They took me with them. I told them, "I am glad it is over." One of them then asked me if I had money or jewelry; I did. They took the money and jewelry and told me not to go back to the apartment. One of the men took me to his apartment, where he and his wife had a Jewish seamstress. If I gave my clothes to the SS man's wife, he would escort me to Warsaw.

In Warsaw, the stories were terrible. The Jewish ghetto was cut off from water and electricity. I stayed with a friend of the family. She said that she could get me papers, but it would cost a lot. I wanted my parents to save their money for themselves. I decided to leave Warsaw and head to Germany as a worker. The day of my departure was May 22. I was to report to the Janowska camp, where I had previously worked. I worried that someone would notice me, but everyone had changed. We were inspected by the German doctors and in front of laughing Aryan policemen, we had to walk around the room naked. We were eventually put on a train to Germany. One of the other women was also Jewish and we decided to get off the train and take one on our own to avoid any problems. We did, and reached Vienna. There were signs everywhere: "Juden Verboten" (Jews Forbidden). We walked around that night and in the morning boarded the train again. My destination was Oberammergau, Germany. I wound up working for a small hotel. In Oberammergau, there were many groups of foreigners working and food was hard to come by. Italians, Russians, Poles, Czechs and others would come to the hotel begging for food. The work was very difficult cleaning and cooking all day. I had to scrub the floors with a brush and rags. I often had to take trips into Munich to get things for the proprietor of the hotel. On one trip I saw men on the tracks wearing striped uniforms, their heads shaved. I found out that they were from Dachau.

After the War

As time went on, the news became better. In mid-April of 1945, many SS came through Oberammergau. They carried lots of food with them; some even had pounds of coffee, which made the locals all very angry. The locals had been drinking fake coffee for years while the SS had pounds of it. On April 24, 1945, the Americans entered the city. We were so happy to see them. We fed them with food we had hidden from the SS. The war was over.

The foreigners were invited to a party at the American headquarters. I met an American there who spoke German well; he was also Jewish. He suggested that I try to go to Palestine, but if I did that how would I find my family? I headed back to Poland. I was first sent to a Displaced Persons Camp. I met people there who knew family members of mine and had been to places that I had. I was the first female Jew to join that particular camp, and that night we all celebrated with cognac. I also met this very mature looking man, Tom, who was to run a hospital for the people from the concentration camps. He asked for my help. The people were very sick from starvation and from typhus. Helping Tom made me realize how much I cared for him, and we were married.

One day, I heard that my father was still alive. A man had come from Poland and said that my father was back as the Director of the Polish Oil industry, but he had no information of my mother. Tom and I got ready to go back to Poland to search for my mother and his sister. Tom had word that his sister had survived Bergen-Belsen. The whole family had, at one time, been in Auschwitz; Tom's parents were killed and his wife and brother-in-law volunteered for death one day because they couldn't take it anymore. Tom's sister, Irena, and he survived. While in the area, I received a letter from both of my parents they survived. For five months they had to hide in an attic with eleven other people. I have pictures of my parents on the day they left hiding. They were so thin and sick-looking.

Over a period of time, my parents, Tom and I made ready to emigrate to the United States. We arrived in the United States in January of 1947. We had a total of 8 dollars. The years were difficult, but we were happy. We have a daughter, born in Germany after the war, and a son, born in the United States. I went back to school and earned a BA, an MS and a PhD at Binghamton University in upstate New York.

Source: Kaplan, Helene C., *I Never Left Janowska,* Holocaust Library, NY, 1989. Reprinted with permission of the Kaplan family.

CHAPTER 12

Righteous Gentiles

At Yad Vashem, the Holocaust Museum in Jerusalem, there is a small grove of trees planted in honor of "righteous gentiles," those who despite great personal danger helped save Jews during the Holocaust. The following story is about the Gestre family of Mon Doubleau, France. After the war, family members stayed in the Elmira/ Corning area for several decades before moving to North Carolina, where they now reside. Genevieve "Suzi" Gestre and her deceased husband, Robert, have been officially recognized as righteous gentiles by the Israeli government.

In 1942, during the Nazi occupation of France, a Christian family sheltered and saved the life of a nine-year-old Jewish girl, Annette. Annette Rappaport and her parents lived in the same Paris apartment building as Genevieve Gestre's mother Julienne Mousseau. When Mousseau asked her daughter to hide and care for Annette, Mrs. Gestre replied with absolutely no hesitation that she would. Years later Gestre explained, "When a person is drowning, you give her your hand and it was normal and that is what I did for Annette." Annette's mother was taken in a sweep by the Gestapo and sent to Auschwitz. Annette's father became involved in the Resistance Movement and on occasion was hidden by the Gestre family, along with his daughter and one of her young female cousins.

The Gestres presented Annette as a relative; still, everyone in Mon Doubleau knew that she was Jewish. Denunciation of those harboring Jews was a constant threat, but the entire community loved and adopted Annette. This enabled the family to preserve Annette's safety. One morning, when the Gestapo would be searching at the local school for Jewish children, the staff got word to the Gestres to keep Annette home. While the Gestapo did search the Gestres' home, they never found Annette or her father.

Consequences meted out by the Gestapo to those who assisted Jews were deportation or immediate death. One family friend found harboring a downed English pilot was sent to Birkenau. She, however, was allowed to survive and return to Mon Doubleau because the Nazis were less punitive with those who aided non-Jews, as compared to the fury they unleashed on those who protected Jews.

At a 1994 ceremony held to honor the Gestre family, a 60 year-old Annette expressed her thanks:

"On July 16 of 1942 (there was a big Gestapo raid on Paris), at which time 76,000 Jews were deported from France, among them 11,000 children. I should have been one of them. Suzanne Gestre always treated me like her own daughter. She was always happy and very optimistic. She was very resourceful in this time of great need. Suzanne was able to make these wonderful pastries out of potatoes.

"Suzanne and Robert risked their own lives (for the sake of) hiding a Jewish child, but they chose camps and they chose the camp of honor. During the years of 1943 -44, they also saved my father.

"I also want to remember the mother of Suzanne, who took it upon herself to go to visit my grandmother, in a home for the aged, where she brought her food and visited her until she, too, was taken by the Nazis."

Source: Comminos, Susan, *The Reporter,* Binghamton, NY, November 3, 1994.

CHAPTER 13

Doris Zolty

The following memoir by Doris Zolty, prepared with assistance from her grandson Jeffrey Wiesner, is the first of three accounts by concentration camp survivors in this collection. Mrs. Zolty was in a number of concentration camps including Auschwitz and Bergen-Belsen. This is the first time she shared her story with the public.

Life Before the Camps

I was born in Garbatka, Poland, a beautiful resort area where, in the summers, about two thousand people would come from all over the country to vacation. The mild air also attracted those recovering from tuberculosis. Both my parents were raised in Garvolin, a large city in Poland, and moved the two hours traveling time to Garbatka after they were married.

My father was a tailor. He did his work in our house, which had three large rooms and front and back porch. I remember my father sectioned off a part of our front porch, and put in a bath for anyone seeking shelter. There were many poor vagrants who wandered from city to city, sleeping in the woods or wherever they could find a place. He was not a religious man, at least compared to my mother. Living the lifestyle of a soldier, during his three years in the Polish army, made a return to observance impossible for him. To live in Poland as a Jew was not easy. I remember one incident that showed the general attitude toward Jews. There was a Jewish man who made his living selling ice cream to the vacationers. He would go door-to-door, or to those picnicking in the woods, and sell out of his small wagon. One day, the church in town held an outdoor party under a pavilion and the ice cream man went there to sell. When he entered, he was approached by the priest and given a slap across the face. It was forbidden for Jews to attend church functions.

On September 1, 1939, when I was nineteen years old, the war began. It did not come as a complete surprise; there had been talk of war since Hitler came to power in 1933. We knew Jews who had been thrown out of Germany. One such family bought the house across the street from us.

We knew war had begun when we saw Polish troops scurrying around outside. When the bombs began to fall, we fled to a farm nearby; the Germans avoided bombing farms because they needed them to produce food. We stayed on the farm for a week, watching the German planes fly overhead. Sometimes if a woman was spotted feeding the cows, a plane would make a low pass and gun her down.

When we returned to the city, all the stores had been cleaned out. The only food we had was that which we brought from the farm. A few days later, on Yom Kippur, I remember we were in synagogue and the Germans came in, took out the religious men, cut off their beards, and put them to work. The Germans wanted to make sure the Jews worked instead of prayed on the holiday. Just to hear the Germans walk made my skin crawl with fear and their voices, their screams. I could see in their faces how much satisfaction they got out of what they did.

In the beginning, the Germans had my father continue to work as a tailor in our home, mending uniforms. But in time he was taken out of the house, every day, to work building roads. At home we didn't say much about the circumstances; just tears and depression. My father's toleration waned with time. One day a German, who had a special dislike for my father, threatened to kill him and ordered him to the police station. My father stopped at home first, to tell us what had happened. I began crying and decided after he left to find out what was going on, to beg for my father's life. During the mile walk to the police station, I prayed to God that if he would let my father live I would believe in him the rest of my life. As I finished saying these words, I rounded a corner where I was met by the chief of police. He knew both my father and me and asked why I was crying. I told him the story, how they had ordered my father to the police station, and how I feared for his life. The chief of police told me to go home where I would be joined by my father soon. So I went home and in an hour my father returned. I remember how he cried. At this time, without hesitation, people were shot all the time.

For the next year and a half to two years, we learned to work for the Germans. I cleaned houses. They took us in the morning and did with us as they wished. We were their slaves. But at least, after work, we were able to come home.

In 1941, we were taken from our homes and placed within a fenced-in area in the center of town: the ghetto. A Jewish police force was established to ensure no one left the ghetto. A police officer failing to stop someone from trying to leave would be shot.

In the ghetto, my family and I lived in a single room, where my father also worked. My grandparents lived in another. We had little food and I became sick with typhus fever. To help me, my father escaped from the ghetto to a farm and brought back a chicken for soup, and some milk. If he had been caught, he would have been shot immediately.

Sometime in 1942, on a Friday morning, the Nazis entered the ghetto and began shooting the men. My grandfather was praying as he did each morning, so I went to warn him to stop. I told him that the SS did not like people praying. He told me that if they were going to kill him, to let them do it right where he sat. The Nazis came in and shot him right in front of me.

The Nazis murdered a seventeen year old girl; they murdered my cousin Fella's seventeen year old brother; they murdered my uncle, a police officer, when he objected that another man had been killed for no reason. In all, fifty-eight men and one girl were murdered. The remaining men were taken to Auschwitz. I never saw my father again. The women were told to dig a large grave and bury the fifty-nine dead.

The Camps

One week later, all the women and children, including myself, were ordered outside to the middle of the ghetto and put in front of a firing squad. Moments before we were to be shot, the Nazis received an order not to shoot us. Instead, we were all to be taken to another ghetto, in Pionki. Soon after our arrival there, we were divided up. My cousin Fella, her other brother, about twenty women, and myself were to be taken to the concentration camp, Pionki. The night before I was to leave, I ate dinner with my mother and she said to me, "Eat, my child, this is the last meal we will eat together." And that was it. I never saw my mother again. She was taken, along with the others in the ghetto, to either Madjdanek or Treblinka; probably Treblinka.

Soon after I arrived at the concentration camp Pionki, I became very sick. The separation from my parents devastated me, I was an only child. I knew that I had a fever, but I was afraid to tell anyone. Since I was unable to work, my boss, Glowacky, discovered I was sick.

He did not report me. Glowacky was married to a girl from my home town Garbatka (Pionki was about 15 kilometers away), so he knew me through my father, his in-laws' tailor. Because Glowacky liked my father, he told me to keep silent about my illness and took me to a doctor. I found out that I had typhus again.

We returned from the doctor and it was made known that I had typhus. Meanwhile, there was another girl who had spit up blood during a typically rigorous work day. Both of us were told that we would be taken to a hospital in the ghetto of Cogenitsa, about 16 kilometers away. This was very strange, to say the least, and we were skeptical. We were taken in a truck by a Verschutz (Ukrainian soldiers who worked for the Germans) named Glubisch, who was an officer, and by a man named Kaplan, who was the head of the Jewish Government in the camp to Cogenitsa.

Glubisch and Kaplan informed someone in the ghetto that I was very sick and should be put into a hospital. Before Glubisch left, he told me that when I was well I should call him and I would be returned to Pionki. Even stranger than being brought to a hospital and the offer to be picked up, was the fact which I found out later that fifty-eight people in Pionki, both men and women, were brought to Dunity (Dunity was the place where people were shot into mass graves) because it was suspected they had contracted typhus from me.

I lay in the hospital, but received no care. The girl I had come with died next to me after a couple of days. I awoke a few days after her death, not feeling any better. Since I wasn't being cared for, I wasn't even getting food, I decided to get up and see what was happening in the ghetto. When I went outside, the trains were standing ready to transport the thousands of Jews out of the ghetto. I left the hospital at around ten in the morning. By two o'clock everyone in the hospital had been shot. Extremely frightened, I remembered what the Ukrainian officer told me: that if I got better I should call him and he would have someone return me to Pionki; it was like a dream, like a ridiculous fantasy, to think in this way. But I figured I would tell the ghetto official. The only problem was getting to him through the thousands of people. I could hardly stand, as I hadn't eaten, but I pushed my way through to Bronsztein, the ghetto president. I saw him sitting at a table with another man, and I told him I needed to speak with him. I remember Bronsztein's retort, "What do you want! Look at what's going on in here, and I'm going to speak with you?!" The man who sat at his side rejoined in Yiddish, "If you can rescue one Jewish soul, then rescue it." So Bronsztein gave me his attention. I explained that I had come from the camp at Pionki, brought here by a Verschutz who told me to call him to be picked up when I felt well again. Bronsztein looked at me like I was absolutely crazy. But he asked how many people were in the camp, to which I replied about 500. Bronsztein took the phone and called the camp at Pionki and asked to speak to the Verschutz Glubisch. Bronsztein asked him to take a few hundred people if the camp had enough room, in exchange for plenty of the gold and diamonds people still possessed in the ghetto. The next day trucks came and took 500 people from the ghetto, including Bronsztein and myself.

When I returned to Pionki, the people there could not believe I was still alive, let alone that I had been taken to a hospital. They figured that I had been shot.

I was still sick but determined to shake it off. I could either be sick and die, or pull myself together, begin to work and perhaps survive. Bronsztein became a Jewish official and treated me very well. For instance, he gave me a special place to sleep, which amounted to having a sheet between my bed and the one adjacent. If I needed a favor, he would grant it to me. If he hadn't been able to go to Pionki, he would have been on a train to either Treblinka or Madjdanek perhaps to Auschwitz.

I remained in Pionki for about two and a half years. I worked digging foundations for new buildings. After work I would return to the barrack and have a little soup, or whatever there was to eat. And then I would go to sleep on my top bunk bed. I did not want to see or talk to anyone. In Pionki there weren't too many restrictions. The guys would often come to speak with the girls and in this way the camp resembled a ghetto. We were needed to work. The bosses were mostly Polish. The Ukrainians worked at the guard station one had to pass through to get into the camp.

Six months before I would be transported elsewhere, about 500 more people came to Pionki from Kelce, a large Polish city. Among those 500 was Sol, the man who would become my husband.

When I began to become acquainted with Sol, I discovered he had little luck; he was beaten up every day passing through the station. He was a carpenter and worked for the Verschutz, constructing shelving where the soldiers' clothing was kept, or whatever else needed to be built. One Verschutz, named Jusczak was a killer. One day he asked Sol for his boots. They were a beautiful pair of boots he had gotten from the ghetto, where a lot of stuff was left around. I do not know the purpose for him asking for the boots, since if he wanted them, of course, he would get them. But he asked Sol to give him the boots and he would give him something else to wear. Sol gave him the boots and received from the shelf a soldier's undershirt and some old shoes. When Sol left on his way to pass through the station, Jusczak called the guards and told them to keep watch because a shirt had been stolen and the thief should be hanged. Sol went through the station and was arrested.

By this time, Sol and I had gotten to know and become fond of one another. When I returned from work I found out that Sol would be hanged; the gallows had already been set up. I needed to find a way to help him. There were some Jews, clothing makers, artisans of all sorts, and artists, who were closer to the Germans because their abilities were valued. These people had influence with both the Germans and Ukrainians. Someone suggested that I go and speak to a man named Hoffman and ask if he could possibly help. A gifted artist, Hoffman worked for the top Germans. I ran to see him and sat upon the floor crying and pleading that he do something to help Sol. Sol was a craftsman, a cabinet maker, and Hoffman liked him. He told me he would try to do something for him. Hoffman went to Glubisch and offered him a fortune to let Sol go. The Jews still had their money. Until going through Auschwitz, Jews still had many of their possessions. Glubisch agreed. Five minutes delay and Sol would have hanged. In Pionki there were many that hanged. They often hanged three people at a time and left the corpses for three days, forcing everyone to look. After the war we discovered that Glubisch was a spy for Russia, which explains why he brought me to a hospital, brought the 500 from the ghetto in Cogenitsa to Pionki, and saved Sol. Later on in 1944, after I had known Sol for one and a half years, we promised each other that if we lived through the war we would marry.

Auschwitz

In May of 1944, we were herded into train cars. I do not remember exactly how long we traveled, perhaps three, four, or five days, and I didn't know our destination. I was still young and I was naive. A hundred people were packed into each car. Sol was among the hundred with me. The lack of ventilation made the heat unbearable. There was no bathrooms and people relieved themselves where they stood. Many people, Sol included, knew where we were headed; there was an underground through which information was circulated.

We arrived at Auschwitz. The first thing I noticed was music from an orchestra. It sounded like we were going to a wedding. With Sol still at my side we were taken to the crematoria. I was completely confused upon seeing the hundreds and hundreds of sacks piled up, filled with what I thought was flour. I figured we were standing outside of a bakery. I asked Sol what they would be baking here bread? Sol responded that it was not flour; the sacks were filled with the ashes of my parents.

Immediately after, Sol was beaten up (he was beaten up so many times), and taken away because he should not have still been with me. I was taken with the other women to a barrack.

On the first, second, or third day I do not remember (I do not want to remember Auschwitz) we were taken to a huge building filled with thousands of people. We were ordered to take off all our clothing and to leave all our possessions. We moved through a line waiting to have our heads shaved. We left this building completely naked and were taken to a place to receive clothing. Tall people received short clothing; short people received long clothing. The Nazis did everything they could to take away dignity.

The following morning they assembled us to be counted. We stood outside naked to be scrutinized by Dr. Mengele. His white uniform and white gloves and the stick he carried remain vivid in my mind. The stick he used to point, "Here, here" to the left, to the right. If my body had a single red mark on it, any sort of blemish, I would have been sent to the crematorium. Whomever Mengele liked, whoever looked young and healthy, went to the right. Whomever he disliked went to the left. All of us were taken to the gas chamber.

The gas chamber was a tremendous room, in the middle of which there was a platform with chairs upon it; shower heads lined the ceiling. Those who had been directed to the left—those who would end up in the crematorium received gas from the shower heads. Those who had been directed to the right sat in the chairs on the platform and received water. I was among the latter, and would go to work. After the shower we left the building and received clean clothing with blue and white stripes and wooden shoes. We were then taken to be tattooed. I became number A-15136. We then went to a very large barrack with three or four bunks to each bed. A couple days later, I was taken along with 500 healthy young girls to Hindenburg, a work camp close by. At this time I did not know where Sol had been taken. I learned later he had been taken to a camp about 100 kilometers away.

There was a German captain named Brown in Pionki. He was a pilot and largely responsible for conquering Pionki when the Germans first raided Poland. He was very good to us. After the war we found out from Kaplan, the top Jewish official at Pionki, that Brown had written a letter to someone at Auschwitz saying that they should not kill us all. He told them we were good workers, and therefore good for the Germans.

In Hindenburg, the threat of being sent back to Auschwitz always hung over us. The camp was new. We were divided and placed in barracks according to the type of work we would do.

I worked in an iron factory where hand grenades were made. Twelve hours a day I polished grenades with a machine, and was required to fill three barrels with three hundred grenades each. Every day I left work black from soot.

Pictures of Auschwitz today, "Work Makes Free."
Photos courtesy of Dr. William Pine

The factory operated all night and normal Germans also worked there. During another shift a German worked at my machine. Sometimes I came to work and found a sandwich wrapped up for me. Other times one of three barrels I was required to fill would be partway filled to make my day a little easier. There was also a soldier in Hindenburg, a redhead, who came from the Wehrmacht, the regular German army. By 1944, the SS were recruiting normal soldiers into their ranks. Every day this man would steal a loaf of bread to give to us when we changed in the factory before work. Daily, he risked his life.

The head of the camp was a man named Tauber. In Auschwitz he was an infamous killer, known for kicking people to death; he knew where to kick, especially the men. Then we left Auschwitz for Hindenburg, those who knew that Tauber would be in charge there pitied us. After the war I had a friend named Rose who spent four years in Auschwitz and survived, yet was very psychologically disturbed. Rose knew Tauber and recalled the way he kicked people to death.

It is bizarre, but Tauber was very good to us in Hindenburg. We lived in barracks kept so clean we could have eaten off the floor. The beds were spotless. We were fed three times a day. I remember once Tauber came into our barrack in the winter and asked us if we were warm enough. If not, he offered to put in another stove.

Hindenburg was a female camp. The kapos were Jewish women from Czechoslovakia. They were very beautiful, but they were killers, often worse than the Germans. Their job was to report who was good and who was bad; who worked and who did not, and who should be killed and who not. The head kapo constantly went to Tauber reporting people for infractions in order to win his favor. As punishment, Tauber had us sit on our knees in the snow for hours after our twelve hour work day. But he hated this kapo and was intent on silencing her persistent reports of our offenses. When Tauber caught this kapo doing something wrong, he beat her violently with the horse whip he carried, and ended her reports.

We stayed in Hindenburg for six months working very hard. On the first of January the Russians came close to Hindenburg. The whole camp was taken on what later became known as a death march. For the next eleven days we would walk through the snow in wooden shoes. The only food we had was the few pieces of bread we brought from Hindenburg. For water we ate the snow. Hundreds dropped to their death along the way. We were first taken to Camp Dore to sleep for a night. This camp was underground in the mountains, filled with German dissidents. I remember I was sitting with a friend at Dore, and a German man snuck in and asked my friend to take a piece of paper he had rolled up like a cigarette. The paper was a note to this man's wife. He told my friend that (the friend) had a better chance to survive than he, so if she was ever in Germany to please deliver the note. People did not know that there were camps for Germans. There were many people that didn't follow Hitler.

From Dore we were taken to Bergen-Belsen. There we were placed in barracks that resembled horse stables, a thousand women to a barrack. They were very large, but with a thousand people we had no room to lay down. After a few weeks enough had died to enable us to lie down. We lay on top of the dead. We were given very little food and water. Each morning we were brought outside and counted. The dead were taken out of the barrack and thrown onto a large pile. I lived this way for three months. After three months there were 200 of us left. There was no longer any fear.

On the fifteenth of April, the English came into the camp. A few days longer and I would have died; once you developed diarrhea you soon died. I remember student doctors came in and they didn't know how to handle the starving. They brought us cans of pork and fatty soup. I was selected to bring the food in; I guess I still looked half alive. People were so hungry they began eating the fat and died like flies. I couldn't believe the way these people died. Unable to voice a groan, they just dropped. After the liberation it seemed like more people died than during the war. I could not eat. I really didn't eat anymore. For a long time after I was content with a cracker and a cup of tea. Hundreds and hundreds were taken to the hospital in the city of Bergen-Belsen; I still remember the screams and cries of these people at night. Many were put into the barracks where the Gestapo used to stay.

I stayed in Bergen-Belsen for a few months, planning my future. I was told early on that Sol had been killed when his barrack was bombed. But some time later I was told that Sol was alive and looking for me. He had been liberated in March. I made my way to Sol in Breslow, Poland, and was married October 6, 1945.

Source: Conversation with Doris Zolty, 1995.

CHAPTER 14

Memoir of Auschwitz

Chi Chi Berman provided us with another memoir of Auschwitz, including the infamous Dr. Mengele. Despite her horrible experiences, Chi Chi survived the war, married an American GI and settled in the United States.

I was born in 1923 and my last name was Katz. I lived in a part of southern Hungary-Kisvarda that was close to the border of Czechoslovakia. I grew up in a town that was highly populated with Jews. There were two schools, one Jewish and one public; I went to the public school. After elementary school, I had tutors until I was 18 years old. My father was a Chasid, a talmudic scholar, and an international wine merchant. My mother was from a rabbinical family. My father's name was Mendel and my mother's name was Teresa Halpert. In my family there were five girls and one boy; I was the second oldest. I came from a wealthy and distinguished family. My mother's side of the family was related to Scribner, a famous classic writer of religious works. My family was quite intellectual my mother held weekly literary salons and famous intellects from the surrounding area attended.

Was there anti-Semitism at this time? Yes, I had a stone thrown at me once and I was called a "dirty Jew." However, I did have some gentile friends who, at the time, asked, "How can she be dirty? They have water to wash." My family noticed a tremendous increase in anti-Semitism once Hitler invaded Poland in 1939. My mother worked to rescue Polish children.

She worked with a type of underground that would bring the children from Poland to her. Then, she would give them papers and they would be dispersed into the countryside through a network. The network tried to hide the children in a tannery, near the border, near Budapest. There were about ten children and one married couple with a child. Something happened to them all. Not one of them survived.

When the Germans came into southern Hungary, everyone had to register. Every day there were different directives: one day you had to turn in your radios, another you had to turn in your bicycles. My father's business was okay, because he had business all over the world. In 1938, he was in the United States and he came home for Pesach. In 1939, he was in Washington, DC, and he tried to get his family out, but he couldn't get back home because of Hitler's army marching. We were on our own with our mother. My brother, at 16, was too young to be drafted into the army and my sisters and I were all under 21. Everyone had to start wearing yellow stars. It was a big upheaval for all of us. Everything happened so fast. My mother was a silent partner with a Christian man and asked him to help by hiding the family, but he refused. My mother began to prepare for the worst. She had a extensive art collection, which she sabotaged; she buried the silver and I don't remember what she did with the jewelry. A Ghetto was made in my town. My brother organized friends to dig an underground way out of the Ghetto. He got out and was safe; he brought medication back into the Ghetto. There were no men in the Ghetto. They were all taken for labor camps. People from outlying areas were brought into the Ghetto.

One woman refused to put on the yellow star and hanged herself instead. Many people also killed themselves when they arrived in Auschwitz. In 1944, the Nazis announced that they were taking us there. It was four weeks from the time our town was invaded until they took us to Auschwitz. They took us in a cattle car. It was very dark. I have no recollection of how long it took because it was pitch dark inside. There was death. We couldn't see, but heard only voices, because the Nazis plugged up the windows. When they took us to Auschwitz and opened the door, there was a man standing there with white gloves on. He told you which way to go. I had been holding a baby on the train and, at the door, I handed it back to the mother. If I had kept the baby, I probably would have been killed.

My mother and younger and older sisters went to the left, (selected for death). I had long, flowing hair. One guy in a prisoner's uniform came up and began kissing my hair. I asked him what he was doing. He said he just wanted to touch living hair, saying, "You won't need it anymore.' That day there were so many Hungarian Jews that the crematoriums could not accommodate all the people. A signal was given to Mengele to be aware of the capacity of the ovens. There was a 'deselection,' and my two sisters returned to my side. There was much confusion and yelling and shouting. They took us to disinfection and stripped us. My brother was outside, but during the night, he broke a (barrack) window and came in to see us. He didn't recognize us because of us being shaved and naked. He shouted our names and told us that we should leave everything and try to get out. He left, and it was the last time I saw him. His name was Philip.

Lager C was the women's barracks. There were 30,000 women in Lager C. My sisters and I were together, but the Germans were not to know that we were related, because they would separate us. None of us had tattoos. We always hid when they had the tattooing; we thought we could escape if we weren't tattooed. Our Lager was run by a Jewish woman, a German woman, another woman named Gretha, and Mengele. Other prisoners, men, came during the day and stood there while we sorted the clothes that we had brought with us. Later, we washed these and they were sent to the Germans. We had to shake every piece of clothing for jewelry. They watched us, but I stole some things anyway.

When our hair started growing back in, it was a very big deal. During air raids, the Germans would leave us alone. Then I would take out the jewelry and combs I had stolen and put them in my hair. During the night, I used to go out and trade jewelry for bread with the kitchen commando.

Once there was a concert, musicians played and the Germans took pictures. They also once gave us postcards to write home. I think I saw some of- these postcards in a museum later.

While the selections were going on, I wore a band on my arm that said I worked in the wash room. Sometimes we hid in the bathrooms during the selection. At first during selections, people ran, but then they closed people up inside so they couldn't run. Sometimes they

Picture of Auschwitz today. Photo courtesy of Dr. William Pine.

counted us twice. One day, during a selection, I had to go to work so I avoided the selection. Almost every second day, they emptied out the sick people. So, I would go out to fetch the water at that time. If I saw somebody sick but who could walk I went to that person and said, "Here's the pail;" and "Come with me." I don't know how it was possible that I could do this. I had to stop it, because once I gave the pail to somebody, and (sigh) Mengele saw what was happening and shot her. For some reason he didn't shoot me. He might have thought that the girl wanted to take a drink from the pail, so he didn't shoot me. I stopped doing those things.

One night, they took us to the crematorium. My sister was screaming. But, as we got closer, it was discovered the crematorium was too full. I remember that I probably said Kaddish. That night they marched us, then took us on a train. We went north; it was all woods, nothing but woods. My sister began to say that they were going to shoot us. They didn't. We set up a camp there. We brought evergreens from the woods to use as beds. We stayed at the camp for two weeks, as a work force, digging ditches. When the guards weren't watching, we didn't dig. It was very cold. One day the Germans took us from the camp and burned it. We walked. It was January of 1945. We had nothing to eat. Every night, they took us to another barn. One night they took us to a barn that only had hay inside. I broke a window there and got out. The farm had a Polish person running it; I begged him to hide us. He refused to help. The next night I did the same thing, and the same thing happened. I knew something was going on. We always had a relay of people who had to pull a wagon at the back of the line. It was my turn to do it. I said I had to see what we carried and opened a box. Inside, were all kinds of clothes for the Germans to wear and all kinds of food for them to eat. The German soldiers told me that the Russians must not be allowed to get it. We had been eating what peasants dropped on the road for us, frozen carrots or whatever. My sister had no shoes.

That night, my sisters and I decided that we should try to escape. The next day, I stepped out of line and went into the woods where I saw a house with a frozen milk pail outside I knew this meant that there was no one home. One sister hid in the chicken coop. The Germans came with dogs to find us, but couldn't smell her because of the chicken smell. After the Germans went away we lit a fire. Poles came during the night and wanted to ransack the house; we kept them away, but they wouldn't tell us what was going on.

During the night, the lights went out and we heard shooting and bombs going off. In the morning, at 0700, we heard the rumbling of tanks. My sister started crying and said that the Germans were coming back. She ran out of the house without shoes and in just a shirt. The tanks were American tanks. A Jewish soldier said "You are safe," and gave us food. The soldier stopped the entire regiment to talk with us.

We stayed in the village till we exhausted all the food. We took care of the cows and people the Russians had left behind. Later we were told to go home, but where was it? Survivors started marching. We went to Odessa. We started to claim that we were Americans, since our father was in the United States. In Odessa, there were American POWs, and five officers from America to escort the POWs home. There were all nationalities there Russian officials interviewed me and said that it would be impossible to get to America. We got to know some of the POWs; one of them, a British guy, tried to help us get together with the Americans. He introduced me to the Americans: four MDs and an officer. Their job was to examine American troops and anyone claiming to be an American. The officer said my sisters and I could go to America. He took us to the officers' mess, fed us, and said that he would put us on the first ship out.

One night, this officer came to where we were staying and asked which one of us was the oldest. He then handed over a big package, for the menses. But we didn't menstruate, because they gave us drugs at Auschwitz to keep us from having a period. We also did not have any clothes. The people from the service gave us fatigues to wear. The day a ship came into port, they took us to it in a closed truck. It was a merchant marine ship, which had room for the three of us and an American woman who had lived in Germany. But this person, who was supposed to be the chaperon was a Nazi sympathizer.

The men on the ship were interested that there were women aboard. Mr. Berman (my future husband), who worked with the steward, wanted to separate us putting us at different tables so everyone could socialize. He wanted me at his table. We were on the ship for four weeks; it was a liberty ship, which was very slow. We went first to Baku, where the Russians interviewed us again. Then we went to the Dardenelles, and on to Istanbul. The Red Cross took the 12 POWs off the ship in Tunisia, because the POWs complained when the captain of the ship asked them to stand watch.

We docked in Newport News, Virginia. Immigration met us there. HIAS was contacted, and we were released into their custody. All we had was our father's address; HIAS found our father and called him. He had not known if we were living or dead. Since our father was Orthodox, he couldn't come to get us on Shabbos. So we met him on a Sunday and went with him to Williamsburg, NY. Because my future husband was the only one on the ship who could talk with us he spoke Yiddish we became friends. He asked my father if he could visit me in Williamsburg. My father asked if he was religious, but Mr. Bertnan came from a very liberal background and for that reason my father considered him not Jewish. I often went to a religious bookstore and, without my father knowing, met Mr. Berman there. We told my father that we wanted to get married, but he was against it. We kept meeting in quiet, but one day we ran into my father on the subway. He took me back home, took away my clothes, and prohibited me from meeting Mr. Berman. When my future husband called later and asked when we could meet, I said now and forever. We found a rabbi in the yellow pages who would marry us, got kids from the street to make a minyan, and stopped and bought a ring. My father sent the police after us, but it was too late.

Source: Conversation with Chi Chi Berman, 1991.

CHAPTER 15

Dr. Edmund Goldenberg

Dr. Edmund Goldenberg, perhaps the best locally known Holo-caust survivor in the Binghamton area, has spoken at numerous schools in the Triple Cities area about his experiences. A medical doctor, with a sharp eye for details and ethical dilemmas, he has written an extensive memoir of life in various concentration camps. The following is a condensed version of this unpublished manuscript, carefully edited by Dr. Goldenberg himself.

Early Years

For close to fifty years I have been unable to write of my Holocaust experiences. It's very painful to recall those memories. At last, I have the nerve to begin. I write now because it is crucial that today's generation and all generations to come know what happened during the Holocaust. It is crucial that everyone realize the evil that one human being is capable of inflicting on another.

In 1939, I lived with my family in Krakow, Poland. My parents owned a small store where I sometimes worked. I was also studying to become a doctor. There were rumors about the possibility of war with Germany, but no one took them seriously.

On September 1, 1939, the rumors were validated. The Germans bombed Poland. Our city, Krakow, was spared heavy attack because the city had many historical valuables wanted by the Germans. At the time I worked in a hospital and saw many wounded, with injuries I had never seen before.

There was talk among the Jewish men that we should flee to Eastern Poland. We figured that with France and England joining the war, the Germans would soon be defeated. My father and I fled. We headed to Zloczow, Poland, where we had family. We traveled by foot along the railroad tracks between Krakow and Lwow. It was a poor choice of routes since the Germans constantly bombed the tracks. Planes flew overhead and fired at soldiers and civilians alike, anyone they could hit. I remember walking a lot since, of course, most of the time the railroad could not run. When possible we paid farmers to drive us by horse cart as far as they would. When the train was running we rode it. We paid farmers for any food they would give us; occasionally someone would share their food. Once we slept at a farm and ate raw eggs and milk in the morning. I saw many dead bodies around large towns. Some lay in fields: I walked through a wheat field and saw a young boy lying there as if asleep but as we approached him we saw that he was dead. We finally made it to our family in Zloczow (pronounced Zworchut).

Soon the Russians came in and took over Eastern Poland. They were greeted like saviors. This was a mistake. At the end of their two year occupation they had turned Eastern Poland into a police state. But the year and a half, from October 1939 until May 1941, was relatively peaceful even though there were some arrests and deportations to Siberia. Communication with my mother in the German part of Poland was rare. Rumors were abundant about the danger there.

With help from my family I was able to go to Lwow, to medical school. As a student, I externed in an eye clinic. I did some eye surgery, mostly the removal of foreign bodies. I received my diploma in the school basement during a bomb raid. During 1940 the Russians had become cruel. Many people were sent to Siberia either as workers or, simply, to disappear. Thousands died in Russian slave labor camps, including friends and family members.

Rumor had it that the German-Russian alliance was not going to last. War between them was inevitable. On June 23, 1941, the bombings began. It quickly became obvious that the Russians did not have a chance against the Germans. Realizing this, many people fled the country. I stayed, thinking I could help my parents. It was too dangerous to attempt a trip back east to my father in Zloczow. Messages from him were rare but I knew he was still alive. I decided to try and make it back to my mother, now in a ghetto in Dobczyce, Krakow. Before I could leave, however, I had to find funds. I found a job as a medical assistant in a Jewish clinic, which did not pay but gave me food. There were few patients since people feared being seen in a Jewish clinic. I earned money occasionally helping people move. Some mornings, on the way to work, I was forced to go to a camp, Janowska, to help with construction. I also helped with first aid since they knew I was a doctor on account of the medical badge I wore. I saw many injuries and a few deaths at the camp. The beatings and shootings increased. I had to get out of Lwow, but I didn't have enough money. Finally a kind man who

I had treated, and who also wanted to leave Lwow, found a German willing to smuggle us both to Krakow. After a day of travel, hidden behind some tires, I was dropped off in Dobczyce.

My mother and cousin, Litsi, lived in a room in a farmer's house. I moved in with them. The town accepted me well because I was a young physician. But, because I had just appeared one day, I was there illegally. My mother gave the Chief of Police's wife a piece of jewelry to keep him

Dr. Edmund Goldenberg
as a young student

quiet. Some time later I also gave him some medical advice which assured my safety; he even gave me tips on how not to get caught by the Germans. Food was scarce and things were generally quiet.

One day the Germans posted announcements demanding that everyone hand over gold, silver, jewelry, and furs. Jews and Poles caught hiding these items were executed. Sewing machines were also confiscated to be used in a new factory set up by the Germans. Women, my mother and Litsi included, had to sew garments for the Germans. Our town was a ghetto. There were not strict boundaries, but one could not have traveled to a neighboring town. My Uncle Leon and Aunt Regina were also in town. Their daughter Gizella was murdered trying to hide.

Deportation

In August 1942, the Germans told us we had to leave Lwow; a "resettlement" move they called it. The farmer we had been staying with was ordered by the Germans to transport us. We were told to take only the things we could carry. We gave the rest to the farmer and his daughter. I stayed with my mother and Litsi and another family until the day of "resettlement." There were horrible rumors circulating among the thousand Jews in Wieliczka. We hoped that whatever was to happen to us would not be as bad as the rumors depicted always naively believing that what happened to others would not happen to us.

"Resettlement" began. Nazis separated the sick and the old right away. My aunt Regina was taken out of the column of people. My uncle Leon begged to stay with her; the Germans did not object since he was gray haired and would not have survived. The sick and the old were murdered immediately. Machine gun fire crackled throughout the day. We were taken to a big field. Several thousand of us sat for hours in long columns. German guards changed every hour, the kinder ones would allow us to leave the column to go to the bathroom in a ditch. There were many beatings. The men were separated from the mass of people. I pleaded to stay with my mother but a German said, "You must live." At that time, I did not yet realize the truth of his words. My family left with a mass of people. In my mind, I can still see how they disappeared, a mass of humanity into a cloud of dust. They disappeared forever. I found out later they had been loaded on a train. I was now alone.

We were kept in Wieliczka, where gun shots and screams echoed, for two or three days. Many Polish people thought Hitler was Poland's savior. These Poles assisted in searching out Jews in hiding. We had to dig graves and bury those who had been shot. The corpses of old people, young women, and little children lay around. I saw a young mother with a child laid out between her legs. We were instructed to bury them in a mass grave and then to dig another. The supervisors were Poles, not Germans. I will never forget the young man who said, "Oh well, too bad," holding a gun in his holster with a big cross strung around his neck this to ensure no one thought he was a Jew.

Soon we were sorted out according to the camp where we would be transported. We were loaded into cattle cars for a one or two night trip. In the morning, guards who were German and Ukrainian chased us out of the cars screaming, firing bullets, and snapping whips. It was September 1, 1942. We had arrived at the camp Rozwadow, where we would remain for the next two and a half months. The camp commandant, Schwamberger, gave the orders: "You will obey all orders, walk in lines, do not attempt to run away-there is a death penalty for every offense. Hand over all money and valuables, anyone caught with money will be shot immediately." Jewish leaders to be responsible to Schwamberger for order in the camp were selected. A doctor was ordered to come to the front. I was not quick enough. Another Jewish doctor was assigned and I would have to go to work as a laborer.

On our second day there, work had not yet begun. People walked around the camp, or worked in the bug-infested barracks. The guards, who were Ukrainian, stood by the fence joking and taking target practice at stray dogs and cats. The noise in the camp was constant from people talking, shouting, and arguing, often about food and clothing, often just gossip true and imaginary. We were given soup and bread. They wheeled the bread in a wheelbarrow.

I remember a young soldier who was ranked a Sturman in the German army and another person in his forties named Pstock. Pstock was not 100 percent "pure Aryan" and was very cruel. At times we were ordered to stand at attention and often, at least in the beginning of my time there, people would be beaten or killed for talking or standing out of line. The bodies were wheeled in a wheelbarrow to the corner of the camp and dumped in a pit, the same wheelbarrow they used for the bread.

On the third day we went to work. To the steel mills in Stalowa Wola we half-ran in columns of five to a row, accosted by guards and beaten if we became unaligned. The steel mill was a vast area, with huge mounds of scrap metal along railroad tracks. The mill supplied the nearby gun factory with metal. The work was dangerous and dirty. We were given no protection from the metal, and injuries were common. Those who were skilled built guns in the factory. These people were lucky. They were needed by the Nazis and granted privileges such as extra food. The cold, the lack of food, and the rigor of the work soon made me weak. Malnourished, my legs began to swell. Fortunately I was given a job indoors, using an air hammer to knock out "faults," perhaps coal and coke from steel blocks. Of course, I was given no ear or eye protection. I noticed everyone rapidly became weaker and weaker, stopping to sit whenever possible. I decreased my water intake to offset the swelling in my feet and ankles.

One incident I remember clearly. We were marching through fields when two men bolted out of their row towards the woods, in an attempt to escape. The column was stopped and a couple of guards pursued the men. One was shot immediately. The other was shot later, after he was found with dogs. And the three remaining in the row were also shot. "This will teach you that you are responsible for each other."

On Yom Kippur, the Germans found out that the rabbi from Wieliczka was fasting. After work the rabbi was called out of the assembly, and the Germans announced that for fasting he would be killed. The rabbi was marched in front of the rest of the assembly and shot in the back.

As time went on, people became sicker and weaker from malnutrition and injury. The most common condition, besides those from injuries, was diarrhea from infestation caused by the filth both in the barracks and the latrine. It was forbidden to go to the latrine at night so many relieved themselves in the barracks. Some risked going out at night, and often it was tolerated; at other times people were shot. Because there were no lights in the latrine, excrement was everywhere, which created a horrendous stench and attracted flies.

Due to the increase in disease and injury, another physician was needed and I was relieved from my factory work. It took two days to wash off the dirt that had grown into my skin. After these two days I was clean enough to be shown to Schwamberger. He told me I was to keep the inmates in working condition. I had to make daily lists of the sick by name. Three days was the limit for sick leave. I was told to take care of the sick and not to expect many medical supplies. As a physician I received more food. I believe acting as a doctor at this time saved my life.

From the beginning I worked in the dispensary for up to sixteen hours a day and was often awakened at night. In addition to cleaning and dressing wounds with limited supplies, I would talk, give reassurance, and try to keep spirits up. This was not easy, since I myself had little hope at this time. There were nights I cried instead of sleeping because I felt so helpless. The rule which limited sick leave to three days was a problem, but I learned to deal with it. If people stayed longer, I covered up for them by submitting someone else's name, an offense for which I could have been killed. Schwamberger complained that too many were sick and there were too few to work. Medical supplies were so limited I finally told the elders and Schwamberger that I needed more medicine and dressing. We received a pass to buy what was needed at a Polish drug store. We had to pay with our own money. I am certain that our getting the pass depended on our agreement to buy the Germans chocolate.

Once, a guard brought a tired man in front of Schwamberger's office. We saw him through the window. Allegedly he did not work fast enough. We pleaded with Schwamberger to let him go, that he would become stronger. But he simply said, "Take him away." The guard brought him to the corner of the camp and shot him. Besides guards, Schwamberger had a few Nazi henchmen who did much killing. One man was 18 years old. He was a deranged sadistic murderer. He enjoyed walking by a column of workers standing at attention and shooting anyone that did not please him. One morning a column of workers stood at attention ready to leave for work. I stood with my 3 or 4 sick people. The Sturman began to scream, pulled his gun and shot everyone in the sick column. One of the victims started crying, "I'm not dead yet;" because he was afraid he would be buried alive. The Sturman shot him again. I was left standing at attention. On another afternoon the sick column was ordered into a barn after the workers left. The Nazi, Pstock shot them all. Perhaps they wanted to convince people not to get sick.

The cold and wet Polish autumn arrived. We hadn't enough clothing or food; sickness, death, and murder decreased our numbers. Apparently, some of the German managers in the steelworks noticed there were a number of good workers and craftsmen, so one day a German chose less than two hundred stronger men to go to the other camp (Stalowa Wola), at the factory. I was one of those chosen. Twelve hundred people entered Rozwadow in September. By the middle of November, fewer than three hundred were still alive. In the camp Stalowa Wola, as in Rozwadow, I was required to report the number of sick. The Sturman was with us the first few days and in these days I reported 22 sick. The next day, the Sturman came with several guards and requested the sick. On this morning, only 21 were present. The Sturman put me in the column and announced that we would all be shot. I was quite resigned, but someone in the camp found the missing man. I was taken out of the column and everyone else was shot. I was beaten on the head. The Sturman left the camp shortly after this incident. The murder of these 22 was the last random execution at Stalowa Wola for the next year and a half, unless someone tried to escape. We had a new commandant, a German, who was relatively kind. The camp was quiet and things became routine: we went to work and we were fed. The three day limit for sick leave was no longer strictly enforced.

We were again working with scrap metal. The work was difficult and we did not have the proper clothing for the cold until the commandant got us what was needed. Large shipments of clothing came in. I assume it was from Auschwitz or another extermination camp. There were heartbreaking notes sewn into the insides and also some money and jewelry.

We never went hungry in Stalowa Wola. We had bread, potatoes, horse meat, and turnips. The potatoes were buried to preserve them, and they often froze. When potatoes freeze they become sweet. To this day, I cannot stand to eat sweet potatoes. Many Poles, who were not residents in the camps, worked with the Jews that were. They brought their own lunches and often shared their food.

The barracks were large, not well lit, and very cold in the winter. People gathered by the wood stove for warmth. I lived in a room with my medical assistant. One room housed the sick. When the workers returned from their workday I always had much to attend to: fever, headaches, bruises, cuts, etc. Luckily I smuggled in a needlelike instrument used to remove corneal foreign bodies from the eyes. I also believe that I used novocaine for eye drops. I must have saved many eyes because I recall removing hundreds of particles.

During the second year, the camp received another transport of people. The Germans needed more workers. Soon after this new group arrived, the children and those gray haired among them were shot. Those who worked as mechanics had much more contact with Polish and even German workers. It was through them that we gained information about happenings at the front lines.

There was a plant dispensary outside the camp where I was permitted to go. Some of the Polish people were kind. One in particular, a secretary, suggested that I write to my father and she would receive the answers. I received about two letters, but then I was caught and taken to the Gestapo. Because I was the only doctor I was not punished. The secretary returned to her home in northern Poland and suggested that I run away and hide in the woods. I was afraid. Because of the distance, it was likely I would be caught. Also I was the only physician and felt needed. I discussed it with the others in the camp and they urged me to stay. A short time after, I was contacted by the secretary in a most unusual way. She had a friend who was a telephone operator in Stalowa Wola, who did the secretary a favor and connected her to the camp. There was a phone in the guard house and, because the Ukrainian guard owed me a favor, he allowed me to speak for a few minutes. I received a long distance phone call in the concentration camp!

I had the opportunity to speak with many people. They came to me not only because of illness or injury but often just to talk. They wanted to express and share their worries and their anxieties. Many suffered from depression they were very pessimistic about their chances of survival. Others spoke about their families, with the hope they were still alive even though it was a near impossibility. They spoke about how it was before the war: how they lived; their homes; their jobs; their hobbies. It was heartbreaking to listen. Though I had little hope myself, I tried to give all the support I could. I felt this was a great responsibility for a person only 25 years of age. One of the most common discussions was about religion and God. I often participated in these conversations. Some came to the conclusion that there was no God. Others thought that we were being punished; for what, they could not say exactly. People were often left torn and upset.

In the final weeks at Stalowa Wola, the whole camp was contemplating escape. There were meetings at night where plans were made. People brought information about where there were woods to hide in: how to split into groups and how to make a hole in the fence. There was great enthusiasm. Unfortunately, things took a sad turn. The plant was bombed. A few died and several were wounded. Several days later, about half the camp escaped. Most were successful. Some were caught and brought back. They were given a stern warning but were not killed. I did not go with them because there were wounded I could not leave behind as they certainly would have died without me. During the last few days of the camp the guards became very kind. They must have known it was the end for them. I recall one incident where they beat a Polish person for abusing a Jewish worker.

We knew the Germans were losing the war and hoped they would leave us behind. They still thought they could win. We were brought to Camp Plaszow, near Krakow, Poland, in cattle cars. The trip took about three days. The camp was large, a few thousand people. People were working and it was very busy. There were few restrictions, and most were not enforced. I became a member of the fire brigade, since there were too many doctors. Luckily there wasn't a fire. We didn't have the proper equipment with which to put out a fire. We probably would have been burned.

Most of the time the camp was peaceful, other times we were beaten. There were gallows, but in the two to three weeks I was there they were not used. Outside the camp there was a hill, visible from every point in the camp, where daily we witnessed executions. There were dug graves and the victims were forced to walk into them to be shot. It was toward the end of the war and the Germans were burning the bodies with gasoline. The smell of burning flesh would stay with me for many years after.

I remember a group of good-looking Jewish women that were brought in to be used for sex by the Nazis. When the Nazis were told they would have to give up their pleasure, they brought the women to the hill and shot them. Everything became more tense by the day. Some tried to escape; food became scarcer; and air raid alarms became more frequent. Gun shots clapped in the distance.

And then one day we were loaded into 18 to 20 cattle cars with 100 people to a car. There was room only to stand. When tired, you could sit with your legs crossed. A few fought their way to the small window in the corner of the box car and begged the guards for a little water. A couple people bought, with hidden money, small cups for ridiculous amounts. The only place to urinate was between the floor board cracks. The stench was unbearable from the sick and the many that had died. When we stopped at certain stations, the guards allowed us to throw out the dead bodies. We tried to figure out where we were going. Some hoped we would be bombed and taken out of our misery. After three days, we ended up in Mauthausen, Austria.

With much screaming and whipping we were unloaded from the train. It was the beginning of September and the weather was cool. We had been reduced to animals. Austrian civilians stood by and watched. We were marched to the camp. As we passed by the women's barracks, they looked for familiar faces. These women were kept by the Germans as prostitutes. These women saved their lives in this way. Every camp kept women for this purpose.

We had to strip naked to be inspected; many were beaten. Finally, they gave out water, which produced mass hysteria since most had nothing to drink for three days. The Germans turned on the fire hydrant full force and everyone ran, trying to drink a few drops. I was able to get a little in my hands to drink. My only thought was how wonderful the water tasted after having none for three days. After much yelling and beating, we were arranged in columns and led to the barracks. We slept in large rooms, on uncovered wooden floors. We were given uniforms and wooden shoes. Our heads were shaved except for a stripe down the middle, for easy recognition if we tried to escape.

A few days later we began work. We were marched along the edge of a quarry. The option to jump was always open to us. If someone did jump, the other prisoners had to carry the body up the quarry. Our job was to walk down almost 200 steps and then carry up big rocks on our shoulders. Other workers broke them up to for roadway paving. On bad days, the guards forced us to run up the steps. One day a guard thought my stone was too small and beat me on the head until it began to bleed. I saw a guard force a prisoner to crawl under barbed wire, while another guard shot him for attempting to escape. Occasionally, a weaker worker who "didn't do his job" was forced to jump into the quarry to his death. At times, whole transports were forced to jump. Mauthausen, like Auschwitz, was an extermination camp. They killed there as fast as they could. The stronger people went to labor camps, which were almost as deadly, so a new work force was needed constantly. There was a crematorium in the camp working constantly.

Many who appeared strong were selected to go to a work camp. We heard rumors that Germany was losing the war, but they dragged us anyway to a camp in the city of Melk. I was only in Mauthausen for 2 to 3 weeks. In Melk, all we heard were screams from beatings and torture. We were divided and placed in barracks, each with several kapos, some of whom were worse than the Nazis. The Germans rarely came into the barracks; they were probably afraid of the filth, and the lice. There was an epidemic of scabies, for which I believe we received medication. I was infested with them and it is fortunate that I improved so quickly. Our work was to dig tunnels in a mountain. We had to haul out dirt and line the tunnel with cement. The tunnels were used to house machinery to provide protection from Allied bombing.

There were a few hundred people in each huge barrack at Melk. In the beginning there were two to a sleeping space, which at first was lined with straw. The straw was soon removed, as it was lice infested.

Before and after work we stood and were counted. If the count was off by one, the thousand people or more would have to stand until the dead body was found in some corner. The dead were supposed to be carried to the count. In the tunnels we had to shovel cement up two layers of scaffolding. We had to take a shovel full of cement and throw it exactly in front of the worker the next level up. If we didn't do it right, we were beaten. Occasionally we had to carry 60 pound sacks of dry cement on our shoulders to the work area. It was very cold with only wooden soled shoes and our uniform. Once during the assembly, a young boy who had tried to escape was paraded through the camp, forced to exclaim how happy he was to be back and then he was killed.

I saw people standing a foot from an electrified fence. They had to stand at attention for hours. Some ended their misery by touching the fence. I remember seeing charred bodies hanging there. The Nazis had whips and put people over barrels to beat them. The victims had to count out loud every blow to twenty-five. They had unbelievable skin wounds and had to go to work afterward or they were killed.

Our shoes became a big problem. Many developed ulcers and infections on their feet, making it very painful to walk. In winter, severe frost bite was very common. If we lost our shoes we had to go barefoot. I could not describe my feelings or thoughts during those months. I did not think rationally. My only thoughts were to wake up in the morning, have the cup of hot, black coffee, go to work, be as inconspicuous as possible, get the day over with, hope for a short assembly, as they sometimes lasted for hours, and get a few hours sleep. In Melk, for food we received hot black coffee in the morning with a piece of bread, full of wood shavings. At noon, murky water with a potato peel if we were lucky. In the evening, bread and coffee. That was all I ate daily, from August 1944 to May 1945. I was not afraid to die, because I was too numb and weak to fear anything I did not feel. The question was not whether we were going to die or not, just when.

I developed a bad pus-filled infection on my thumb. I kept it to myself for a while, but it became worse so I went to the dispensary. A Greek doctor removed the nail without anesthesia, of course but he saved my thumb. I was in the "hospital " for about two weeks. I didn't have to work but I received less food. We slept four on the upper bunk and four on the lower. On two occasions, I awoke with a dead body next to me. I had the job of washing newcomers to the hospital. Once I washed a nice looking young man who moved slowly and wouldn't get up. I helped him as much as I could, dried him and told him he could go to bed. Then I realized the man was dead-he died sometime during his bath. Everyday the German supervisor came, and whoever looked half alive was sent back to work. Soon it was my turn.

There were groups whose job it was to drag dead bodies out of the barracks and pile them up for a truck to take them to the oven. The bodies were stripped of clothing, and a special group pried open the mouths of the corpses and chiseled out the gold teeth. I saw this done several times. It seemed the German war effort was not faring well. We heard bombings and aircraft every night, possibly the British. Occasionally, we stayed in the barracks; the Germans probably did not want us to witness their defeat. We thought that soon we would be left behind. We were wrong. In late March, they took us to another camp, Ebensee. We left in big barges on the Danube River.

We traveled by boat two days, then we walked for another three days. Many saw us along the way: cargo boats, etc. Many knew of our existence. It seemed like we walked very far. Many died along the way. They could not walk and were shot for it. We dragged those we could. The guards were older and less aggressive. Some talked to us. These guards were not the real SS; they were Volksturm, people taken from communities and placed in uniform for just this type of work. We had less food: occasional water and bread, perhaps once.

We stood for hours at the assembly at Camp Ebensee. It was a new camp and poorly constructed. The barracks allowed the wind to whistle through them. We slept on bunk beds made of wooden planks that sometimes collapsed. The ovens were in operation from the first day. As at Melk, there were always piles of bodies in front of the ovens; they couldn't burn them fast enough. Day and night, the smell of burned flesh hung in the air. We received about the same amount of food, perhaps even a little less. I remember, once, a healthy worker stole a piece of bread out of my hand, that was too weak to hold on to it. I had to spend a terrible 24 hours on water alone. The "soup" was still a murky warm water that often smelled rancid. We had to report to work everyday, but we had nothing to do. We just sat around and listened to rumors about the state of the war.

A few days before liberation, the SS commandant asked us at assembly whether we wanted him to hide us in the mines where we'd be safe from the bombings of the Americans. But we were informed that the entrance to the mine was wired with explosives. The war was just about over, and still the Nazis thought of nothing but finishing us off. The camp was not bombed and the guards had fled. Then, one morning, I heard a loud, "the Americans are here." Everyone ran, crawled, or was dragged outside. Just past the gate, there were two tanks. A crowd of people surrounded them, with arms raised, and crying for food, for water, and for joy. The scene remains vivid in my mind. It was so unreal it was unbelievable. I was too weak to push myself toward the liberators, but I could see four or five soldiers sitting on the tanks crying. To watch them brought forth the first bit of emotion I had felt in a long time. It was the first moment that I began to realize that something very big was happening to us.

There was a big fountain close to the gate filled with water two feet deep. It was difficult to get to it, but I climbed into it so I could drink. I was helped out of the fountain as I would never had made it out alone. I looked back and saw a few bodies floating in the water. This all took place in the late morning. Later we finally got clean water. The Americans were trying to create order. They cooked a kettle of meat stew. The stronger pushed their way in first so it was difficult for me to get any. I faked fainting and was carried to the front of the line to get food. I felt full after eating it, cherishing every bite. Since our stomachs were unaccustomed to such rich food, it was unwise to eat too much; many did and became sick. There were many people whose bodies gave out after only a few hours of liberty. I heard a few dying people say, "We can die happy, we are free!"

Adapted from a memoir written by Edmund Goldenberg and printed here with his permission, 1997.

16

Poems

There were many forms of resistance to the Nazi war against the Jews. Partisans took up guns in the forest and the ghettos. Religious Jews continued practicing their religion even in the concentration camps. Occasionally, even poetry was written and shared. The following poems were given to Rabbi Sussman by a family member who survived Theresienstadt. They speak of suffering, memory and hope.

A Eulogy for a Beloved Soul

Died of hunger at Theresienstadt March 8, 1944.

> Snuffed out is your life so filled with love
> Dear friend who was both mother and child to me
> And I who loved you so much had to remain.
>
> With you at my side, the worst became bearable.
> I wanted to live, I wanted to be there
> In order to help you in your torture and pain
> To support you, to care for you,
> To wait with you, to wait for "tomorrow."
>
> But now the last reason for living
> Has vanished with your death.
> Can you rest now from your misery and suffering?
> Has your soul finally found its home?

Have you been freed from all torture?
Is this life really only a valley of wretchedness
Before ascending to brighter heights?
Will we, at some future date, see each other again?
Is there a beyond? Who can answer our questions?!
And even if death is only a beginning
We still have to live a life full of torment,
A life full of longing and full of anxiety
After all our loved ones, who left us,
Annihilated cruelly and senselessly at the camp,
Crushed by hunger and suffering.
God take my life too.
It's become too difficult.
I'm so alone I'm suffering too much.

Dr. Herta Schellmann
Theresienstadt-March, 1944

Translated by Norbert Adler, April 1994

Poem About The Ghetto Theresienstadt

Theresienstadt, you city of suffering,
How much we had hoped to avoid you.
A city where it's possible even in the most difficult hours
To have some lighter thoughts.
Thoughts nurturing our hope,
That we won't be devoured by suffering.

Theresienstadt, you city of sorrow,
Awakening every morning full of fear
And yet thanking God in our misery

Even though the soup is thin and the bread is scant.

Theresienstadt, Theresienstadt,
What is happening to us here is unforgivable.
Yet your soil is holy to us.
And with deepest pain we remember
The dead we are leaving behind here.

Theresienstadt, when we finally leave
That will mean freedom from the suffering.
And when we are driven apart,
Our memory will remain
Of human hatred and human suffering,
Of goodness and eternal helpfulness.

But once we are free and no longer suffering,
Then at a future date Theresienstadt will just be a dream.

Lilli Pohl
Theresienstadt 194?

Translated by Norbert Adler, April 1994

Excerpt from: Send a Sign of Life

Whenever you leave me
Even for a short time
I cannot deal with the separation,
I am secretly crying.

You never liked to have scenes made
When we said good-bye

On the (railroad) platform.

And I spoke to you in a light vein
Without showing any tears
Please send me a little sign of life soon, darling,
To tell me how you are and what you are doing . . .

Lilli Poll
Theresienstadt 194?

Translated by Norbert Adler- April, 1994

Nachruf für eine geliebte Tote.

Hungers gestorben in Theresienstadt am 8. März 44.

Erloschen Dein Leben, an Liebe so reich
Freundin Du, Mutter und Kind zugleich.
Und ich bleib zurück - ach, ich lieb Dich so sehr.
Mit Dir war das Schwerste mir nicht zu schwer.
Ich wollte leben, ich wollte sein,
Um Dir zu helfen in Qual und Pein,
Dich zu erhalten, für Dich zu sorgen,
Mit Dir zu warten, warten auf das "morgen"
Nun ist der letzte Lebenssinn
Mit Deinem Tode auch dahin.
Ich sehn' mich danach in Nächten und Tagen,
Dir Gutes zu tun, etwas Liebes zu sagen,
Dich, Liebstes, die zarteste aller Gestalten,
Wieder wie einst im Arm zu halten,
Wieder wie sonst keine Mühe zu scheun,
Dich zu behüten und zu betreun,
Dir hier das Leben leichter zu machen.
Ich denk an Dich in all den wachen
Stunden der Nacht, die so endlos sind.
Freundin Du, Mutter, geliebtes Kind.
Ruhst Du von Not und Leiden nun aus?
Fand Deine Seele ein endlich zuhaus?
Bist Du erlöst nun von aller Qual?
Ist dies Leben hier wirklich nur ein Tal
des Jammers vor Aufstieg zu lichteren Höhn?

Werden dereinst wir uns wiedersehn?
Gibt es ein Jenseits? Wer kann es mir sagen,
Wer Antwort geben auf unsere Fragen?! — —
Und sollte der Tod ein Beginnen erst sein,
So bleibt noch zu leben ein Leben voll Pein,
Ein Leben voll Sehnsucht und voller Bangen,
Nach all den Unseren, die von uns gegangen,
grausam und sinnlos im Lager vernichtet,
Durch Hunger und Leiden zugrunde gerichtet. —
Gott nimm auch mein Leben — mir ist es zu schwer,
Ich bin so allein — ich leide zu sehr.

Dr. Herta Schellmann.

Theresienstadt im März 1944.

Handwritten original of "A Eulogy for a Beloved Soul,"
by Dr. Herta Schellmann,
Theresienstadt, March 1944

(The original of this poem is in the possession of Rabbi Lance
J. Sussman)

CHAPTER 17

Sanctuary

By proximity, Binghamton is situated only a few hours drive from the site of the only group rescue resettlement effort made by the United States government during the war. "Sanctuary," an article in the 1944 Center Reporter Yearbook, documents the local community's awareness of the internment camp at Fort Ontario in Oswego, New York. Unfortunately, the rescue efforts of the American government were limited to this one experiment in housing European Jews. Absorption of other independent refugees and immigrants also often proved difficult because of social differences and the exigencies of war.

"Give me your tired, your poor,
Your huddled masses yearning to breathe free,
The wretched refuse of your teeming shore.
Send these, the homeless, tempest tossed to me,
I lift my lamp beside the golden door!"

Given time and setting, words and thoughts have the capacity to enthrall even beyond the range intended by their authors.

To the bewildered refugee, just rescued from the wrath of Hitlerism, the inscription at the base of the Statue of Liberty carried greater dramatic import than perhaps envisioned by Emma Lazarus. Nearly a thousand of them, nationals of seventeen different countries, were admitted into the haven of America on August 3rd. Their temporary home in comfortably improvised barracks at Fort Ontario was made possible by our Government through the War Allocation Authorities.

These weary wanderers represented a fair cross-section of the millions who have been uprooted and made homeless by the Hitlerite "New Order." They personified the mass tragedies of Europe wrought by the "Super-race." Among them were former merchants, artists, students, novelists, physicians. They represented the religious persuasions of practically every known central European faith.

Newspaper reporters, arriving at the destination of the wanderers, recorded varied emotional reactions. Here was a former Vienna merchant proudly telling reporters that his son, for some years a resident of the U.S.A., was fighting the Nazis in the uniform of a U.S. soldier. There was the Rabbi who donned his praying shawl immediately upon being assigned to his quarters and who gave prayerful thanks to the God of Abraham for his deliverance and to this merciful nation for his asylum. He also stood by in respectful and reverent approbation. There was a tearful expression of appreciation by all for granting them sanctuary even if only for the war's duration.

Source: Jewish Center Yearbook, Binghamton, NY, 1944.

CHAPTER **18**

The Binghamton Press 1944-1945

One of the most discussed issues concerning the Holocaust involves awareness of Nazi action against the Jews among the Allies. We now know that the American government knew about the "Final Solution," and did not take specific military action to stop or disrupt it. Information was also readily available in the popular press, as these articles from the Binghamton papers from June, 1944 to the end of the war, demonstrate.

Articles from the Binghamton Press

June 21, 1944- "Germany tries to destroy France."

Figures from the French Committee of National Liberation show this. Prior to WW II the population of France was 40 million. Of this number, one in seven has been uprooted. More than 850,000 French soldiers are held prisoner. 350,000 have been forced into Nazi labor. 900,000 have been deported to Germany. Some 60,000 Jews and saboteurs have been removed from the country to an unknown fate.

July 15, 1944- "Day of Defeat Approaches; Nazis Launch Terror Reign"

A Nazi "reign of terror" throughout occupied Europe was reported officially today to be increasing in savagery as the enemy's desperation grows with the relentless approach of his day of defeat. It was the reported wiping out of the Grecian village of Distomo and mass killings of Jews in Hungary which- prompted Secretary of State Hull today to denounce atrocities anew and to promise that punishment will be dealt out to the Nazi perpetrators. More than 1,000 persons were reported killed at Distomo . . . Of the massacre of Jews in Hungary by the Nazis and their "Hungarian Quislings," Hull declared that the number of victims is already great and "the entire Jewish community in Hungary which numbered nearly I million souls is threatened with extermination."

August 22, 1944- "Nazi Prisoners and Jews"

Observers at Fort Knox, Ky., have been shocked at the way Nazi prisoners have carried their Fuhrer's racial theories into the heart of America. A group of prisoners is assigned to the officers' restaurant at Fort Knox, and make efficient waiters. But whenever a Jewish officer enters, they refuse to serve him.

"We will not serve people of that nationality," they say.

Non-Jewish US officers have taken no steps to change the ideas of these young Nazis, are inclined to treat the matter as a joke.

August 30, 1944- "Newsman Tells of Horror of German Death Factory"

Lublin, Poland. Four German prisoners of war told their stories in front of a Russian Polish Atrocities Commission. They told that men, women and children of 22 different nationalities were gassed, hanged, shot, burned, drugged or starved to death in the three years of operation of Madjdanek, located near Lublin. Until newsmen from America and Britain visited the camp, they had no idea of the crematorium surrounded with skeletons, piles of human ashes mixed with manure for fertilizing cabbage, and its overflow burial ground carpeted with decaying bodies.

"With our clothes still reeking of the stench of death, we sat and listened to the testimony of officers who blamed it all on, orders from above." Herman Vogel, an SS group leader from Muhlheim, stared ahead with a set face as he told of shipping 18 carloads of clothing to Germany from the Madjdanek warehouse he supervised. "Yes, all the clothing... belonged to those executed." He said. "I have seen groups of 120-150 persons taken to the gas house in the evening and their bodies stacked outside the next morning."

SS Obeersturmfuehrer Anton Ternes said, "The camp physicians told me that as many as 300 children were killed in a single day."

The gas chambers were sufficient to kill 2,000 in less than seven minutes. The crematory ovens handled 1,900 corpses in a 24 hour period. The majority of the dead were Soviet war prisoners, Jews and Poles, but every country in Europe was represented, even China.

April 2, 1945- "Freed Yanks tell of Nazi 'Care' Given"

When the US Sixth Army liberated a German Prisoner of War Camp near Siegenhain, Germany, they found 1,277 Americans captured in the Battle of the Bulge. They had lost 25-40 pounds per man in the three and one-half months of a semi-starvation diet. Other nationals were found in barbed wire enclosures in an open field near Siegenhain. The troops included 1,000 Russians, 200 Poles and an assortment of 100 Serbs, Slovaks, Moroccans, Belgians, Senegalese and South African Negroes. The Sixth Army also freed 900 Jewish women between the ages of 16-35 who had been imported by the Germans from Hungary as slave labor. They told of sick girls, unable to work, being stripped, thrown into trucks with dead girls and hauled off and cremated.

Americans reported the Germans stripped them of their watches and moneys. A prisoner from the Midwest said his captors took away his shoes and forced him to march 80 miles through the snow in his stocking feet. One group of prisoners was held in box cars 7-10 days without food and water.

April 25, 1945- "Prisoners at Belsen Camp Endured Continual Torture"

Prison courtyards of Nazi atrocity camps were torture arenas. Dogs were sent to rip the clothes from defenseless prisoners. Naked men and women were paraded together in the bitter cold. A group of women held in Belsen said that tortures flogging of women's breasts, lashing of the soles of feet, forced prostitution, the use of human beings for vivisection experiments were "enjoyed" by Nazi women SS guards as well as German men.

May 1, 1945- "Record of Jewish Soldiers In This War Is Impressive"

Anti-Semites and Germans have stated that Jewish soldiers are not fighting and dying in this war, this is a lie. Millions of Jewish men and women in uniform are fighting in the armies of the United Nations to free all people from oppression and slavery. The following is a list of 'firsts" accredited to Jewish men and women in the Armed Forces of the United States to date in World War II.

First to raise the American flag on pre-war Japanese territory was Lt. Col. Melvin Krulewitch of New York City.

First American penetration of German soil was made by Third Armored division commanded by Maj. Gen. Maurice Rose of Denver, son of rabbi, later assassinated after he had surrendered when he got too far in front of his command.

First three Americans to enter Aachen, the initial German city captured by the Americans, included Pvt. Max Fingelstein of Brooklyn.

First American assault boat to hit the shore on France on D-Day was commanded by Lt. Abe Condiotti of Brooklyn. First Nazi plane shot down for Uncle Sam is credited to Lt. William E. Beck of Nashville, Tenn.

First American Red Cross nurse killed in World War II was Esther Richards, who died of wounds received at Anzio beachhead.

First American Army nurse killed on Western Front was Lt. Frances Slanger, who died of wounds received in Belgium.

First B29 raid on Japan included bombers on which Capt. William C. Goldstein, Sgt. Morris Kramer, and Capt. Stephen Silverman.

First American unit to break through to relieve the trapped American garrison in Bastogne was a tank unit commanded by Col. Creyton Abrams.

First American enlisted man to receive the Purple Heart in continental Europe was Sgt. Irving Allen.

First American League baseball player to join the armed forces was Hank Greenberg, of the Detroit Tigers.

May 2, 1945- "Dachau Liberation Brings Horrible Discoveries" by Howard Byrne

The Dachau crematorium is a long, low brick structure with a tall smokestack from which smoke poured day and night.

The gas chamber is 20 feet square and has 18 nozzles across the ceiling which look like shower outlets.

The resemblance was intended, authorities said. The guards told the murderhouse victims to undress and prepare to shower.

They entered the room nude and when the room was full, the door was shut tight and the gas turned on while attendants watched the death throes through a telescopic device in the wall.

Cremating was done by habitual criminals who were fed well while on detail and promised liberty parole after several months good service.

But the Nazis played a wry joke on their helpers. When parole time came they were pushed into the gas chamber themselves.

Jan 4, 1946- "Order of 5,000,000 Jews on Nazi Orders Disclosed"

The Nazi leadership conceived and executed a program which bathed Eastern, Central and Southern Europe in blood and claimed up to 5,000,000 victims, two SS officers declared today.

Maj. General Otto Wendorf testified that the special SS groups were attached to the German Army when the Nazis attacked Russia with orders to kill every Jew and political commissar in regions overrun. Women and children were not spared, although later, to protect the feelings of those German soldiers who might object, the children were consigned only to gas vans for execution, he said. His orders were that the Jewish population be liquidated in its entirety, including children.

July 23, 1945- "Nazi Leaders Show Nerves on Seeing 'Horror' Movies"

As guests of the United States Army, high Nazi leaders interned here have seen movies of the Buchenwald horror camp and other records of their government's brutality. Sgt. Arthur Michaels, army interpreter, told how some of the Nazis reacted:

Dr. Hans Frank, Nazi administrator of Poland, crammed a handkerchief in his mouth and gagged.

Field Marshal Albert Kesselring was white as a sheet when the picture ended.

Joachim von Ribbentrop, the former Nazi Foreign Minister, bowed his head and walked straight from the showing to the dining room.

September 26, 1945- "Nazis Used Women for Experiments, Polish Girl Says"

The British Military Court was told today that the Nazis practiced artificial insemination of women prisoners. So painful were the experiments that many victims died, those who survived were later killed by blood stream injections of gasoline and disinfectants. The witness also said that weak hospital patients were killed by injections given by SS doctors.

Source: Printed with permission of the *Binghamton Press & Sun-Bulletin.*

CHAPTER 19

Bergen-Belsen and Dachau Photos

*Two soldiers, Philomen Mullins and Leo McNerney, from the Triple
Cities area were present at the liberation of the concentration camps
Bergen-Belsen (4.15.45) and Dachau (4.29.45), respectively.*

Bergen-Belsen, Photos by Philomen Mullins

*They took amazing photographs that they kept in their posses-
sion for years. After their recent deaths, their families donated them
for this book. Mrs. Mullins, the widow of Philemon Mullen, said that
her husband never talked about the liberation of Bergen-Belsen. "It
was too sad."*

Bergen-Belsen,
Photos by
Philomen Mullins

Bergen-Belsen,
Photos by
Philomen Mullins

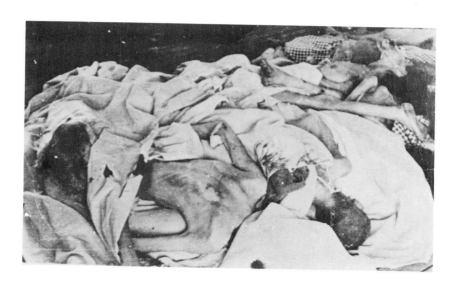

Bergen-Belsen,
Photos by Philomen Mullins

Bergen-Belsen, Photos above
by Philomen Mullins

Dachau, Photos by Leo McNerney

Dachau, Photos by Leo McNerney

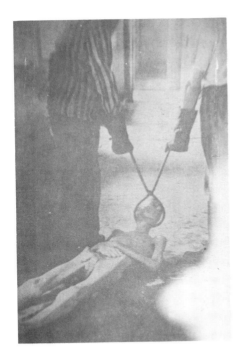

Dachau, Photos by Leo McNerney

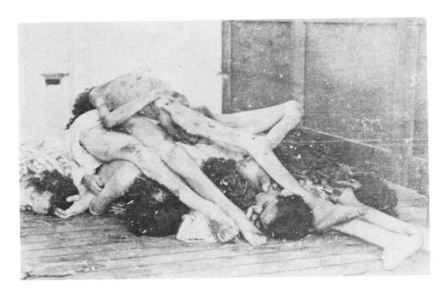

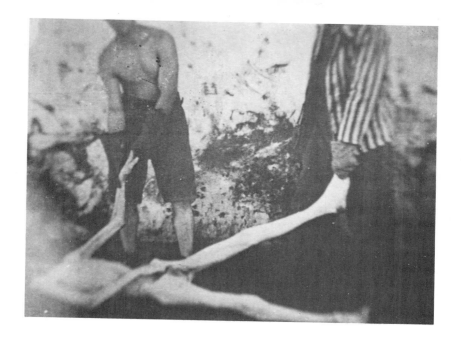

Dachau, Photos by Leo McNerney

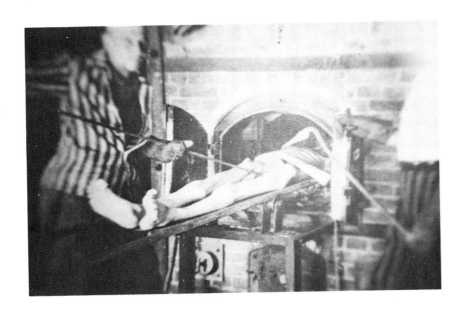

Dachau, Photos by Leo McNerney

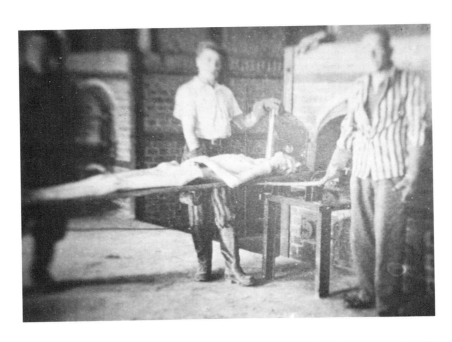

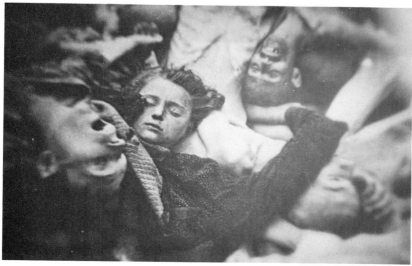

Dachau,
Photos by
Leo McNerney

CHAPTER 20

Liberation

With the defeat of Germany, the enormity of the crimes of Nazism against the Jewish people came into clear view. For the Jewish people, the scope of the losses were unfathomable. In a 1944 article called "Liberation," which originally appeared in that year's annual Binghamton Jewish Center Reporter Yearbook, *the contrast of the liberation of Rome and Minsk was telling. The great centers of East European Jewish life were no more. It is interesting to note that the editorial ends on a highly universal note. Apparently, the war in Europe was not yet over when "Liberation" was written and the conflict in the Pacific continued to rage. With the end of the war, the Jewish community quickly refocused on providing aid and shelter to the survivors of the Holocaust and urging the creation of a Jewish state in British Palestine.*

"Teka b'shofar Godol Le'cherusaynu Ve'sa nes lekabetz Galuyosainu." "Sound a great Shofar for our liberation And raise a banner to gather our exiles."

During the past year, the United Nations has gone a long way toward the liberation of the world from Nazi oppression. The American, British and French forces are racing across France at a fabulous rate of speed toward the "Sacred German Soil," and the valiant Russian Armies have regained hundreds of thousands of miles of Soviet territory devastated by the invader. Two of Europe's great capitals, Rome and Paris, have been liberated and Bucharest may be in our hands by the time we go to press.

The overflowing tide of happiness that welled up in the hearts of the Italian population when the armies of the Allies marched into Rome, not as conquerors, but as liberators, is beautifully conveyed by the letters of some of our own Binghamton boys who had agonized in the mud of Italy for many months. The meteoric joy of the Parisians at their release, after four years of nightmare, is still fresh in our minds. These spontaneous celebrations tell the story of what we are fighting for better than any exposition that can ever be written. Human beings are living again, laughing again, rejoicing again.

Another capital was liberated during the same period, Minsk, the capital of White Russia. We did not read of any spontaneous outbursts of gaiety and hilarity in Minsk, nor of any parades or carousels. Why were not the inhabitants of Minsk as happy to be rid of the Nazi terror? Were not the echoes of the footsteps of their own soldiers sweet music to their ears? No, because there were no ears to hear and no hearts to be happy. Minsk was a dead city murdered in cold blood.

Minsk was virtually a Jewish city. More than 200,000 Jews lived there when the Nazis first blasted their way into it. Exactly six Jews were left alive to greet their redeemers. The rest men, women, and children alike were mercilessly tortured and exterminated by gas chamber or machine gun. This dastardly crime had its parallel in every city in Poland and Russia as it fell into the hands of these scientific barbarians-but never before in the pages of history. For nearly five million of our people, the sun had set, never to rise again. For them, there is no liberation.

The Nazis and their empire of darkness are tottering. They may collapse before the ink on this page is dry. The representatives of the United Nations have assembled at Dumbarton Oaks to draw the blueprint of the structure of permanent peace. We hope that these plenipotentiaries, upon whom the eyes of all the broken-hearted of the world have been resting, will feel these millions of souls hovering about their round table. Let their fate be a grim reminder that no edifice will be stable, unless it has as its foundation the basic right of every human being to life, liberty and the pursuit of happiness. No peace will be permanent unless it safeguards the rights of our people, along with those of all other minorities. Liberation will be a hollow word, until atonement is made for our terrible sacrifices.

Source: Jewish Center Yearbook, Binghamton, NY, 1944.

Bergen-Belsen, Photos by Philomen Mullins

CHAPTER 21

Never Forget . . . Schindler

*The following essay was written by a distant cousin of Elihu
Schagrin, Rabbi Emeritus of Temple Concord, Binghamton. His
cousin, Zacharia, settled in Israel on Kibbutz Barkai, Israel*

*Following his retirement from Temple Concord, Rabbi Schagrin
took a one-year assignment in Melbourne, Australia. While serving
as the Rabbi of the Leo Baeck Center in Melbourne, Schagrin happened across this essay in his office files. No one knew how it got to
the synagogue, how it got to Australia at all, or even who translated
it. But there it was, waiting to be discovered by a family member!*

"Long ago, when I was a child, I remember walking with my father
to the cheder where I was to learn Bible and Talmud. He had a single
request to make of me: 'I am aware,' he said, 'that you won't turn out
to be a Rabbi; but nonetheless, I want very much for you to learn the
Hebrew prayers so that someday, when my time comes, you will be
able to say Kaddish on my grave.'"

"Unfortunately, I never carried out this wish. I did not say Kaddish
on his grave, because never was there a Kaddish written. not then as he
was led away with the rest of my family to the concentration camps and
not now 40 years later that can express the depth of the pain and sorrow
of those who lost all their loved ones in the Holocaust. Never has there
been a Kaddish written for the loss of an entire people, with its millions
of children, ten thousand homes and villages, all disappearing without
a trace.

"Those who survived the inferno have a different prayer, not one that was written in the ancient Aramaic tongue, and not one which promises, 'He who makes peace in the heavens . . . will make peace upon us and His people Israel.' Their prayer, instead, speaks a different language, one of memories engraved in a huge book the pages of which number the days of the German conquest. Their Kaddish is written in the blood and ashes of six million victims, who were human beings and whose only sin was that they were Jews, the 'Chosen People.' And the 'All Merciful' who dwells in heaven did not send his angels to stop the terrible sacrifice and was blind to the smoke rising from the crematoria and did not see His People's rivers of blood as they were slaughtered. And on every page in this book of memories, it is written: 'To remember and never forget.' For, in spite of the fact that 40 years have passed, each page remains clear and the letters are sharply defined. Few remain who can comprehend the 1700 days of the Holocaust, from its inception to the end, when the Nazi beast was finally put down.

"To Remember . . . The childhood days before the Holocaust. The tranquil town with its thriving Jewish population the voices of the children repeating after the rabbi, 'kometz aleph,' . . . The smell of cooking on a Sabbath evening the quiet of the holy days and the walks in the fields and forests the bustling of market days and the calls of the vendors.

"And Never Forget . . . Even then we were afraid to walk down the streets to the taunts of the Polish youth . . . the signs that read, Jews are forbidden entrance, 'Do not buy Jewish products,' and 'Jews, go back to Palestine,...The terror of pogroms and the first knowledge of what was happening in Germany.

"To Remember . . . The outbreak of war and the wailing of sirens the noise of Nazi planes and the panic that gripped us all the thousands of refugees on the roads the escape from our homes, in a huge wave of displaced persons . . . the terrible uncertainty of not knowing where to go . . . the first dead bodies at the wayside, shot down by German gunners. "And Never Forget . . . The sight of the vanquished Polish army moving aimlessly to and fro . . . The Jewish soldier, shot down by his commander as a traitor, perhaps the war's first victim . . . the plundering of the stores and homes of Jews who had run away . . . the Polish welcoming committee, greeting the advancing German army with flowers.

"To Remember The religious old Jews, whose beards were cut off in the street to the laughter of the passersby the first round-ups of Jews to the labor camps . . . the snow we shovelled from the streets of Poland . . . the many and varied 'clean-up' jobs . . . the helplessness and the fear the rules and regulations imposed on Jews the beginning of the fight for existence.

"To Remember . . . The first day at the stone quarries run by Poles . . . the humiliating way they treated the Jewish youth unaccustomed as yet to the hard physical labor . . . working all day, with heavy mallets, loading rocks on railroad cars . . . the day I was injured and staggered home holding my wounded arm, while passersby threw rocks at me and shouted, 'Zhid.'

"To Remember . . . The first transport to the labor camp, bidding farewell to my family and not knowing that it would be the last time I would ever see them . . . the welcoming committee at the camp and the camp commander saying, 'Many people enter this place but no one ever leaves.'

"And Never Forget . . . The group of women put to death in the camp, accused of espionage in the kitchen where they worked, shot down in the dark by Ivan the Ukrainian, an expert at cold-blooded murder .. the woman who was miraculously unharmed and rose to her feet pleading for her life, only to be shot to death in front of our eyes.

"To Remember . . . The whistles of the trains bringing their human transport to the extermination camps . . . the eyes peering out through the barred windows . . . the last sign I received from my family in the form of a note, thrown from the moving train, 'We are all together; take care of yourself.' The last words of my father.

"To Remember . . . The hundreds of dead from the typhoid epidemic that raged through the work camp, all buried in a single mass grave the medic from my village, who found me among the dying and cared for me tenderly, until I was able to stand on my feet again . . . the selection after my illness when we, the living skeletons, were marched in front of camp commander Muller standing with his dog, specially trained to attack Jews in one hand he held a cane, and with this cane he indicated who was to live and who was to die.

"To Remember . . . The touch of the cane on my neck and the shout, 'Raus,' which meant to join those marked for death . . . the last march to the extermination camp, each of us knowing what fate awaited him.

"And Never Forget . . . The miracle in the form of Oscar Schindler, who pulled us at the last minute from the clutches of death, gathered us up, old and young alike, and brought us to his factory in Krakow where he cared for us until we were able to work again.

"To Remember . . . The return visit to my village after the war, seeing it emptied of Jewish life, seeing the shock of the Polish people as they discovered that some Jews still remained.

"And Never Forget . . . Those who were not fortunate enough to survive and be rehabilitated in a Jewish land and share our good fortune THEY HAVE COMMANDED US NEVER TO FORGET."

Source: Zacharia Schagrin, from the *Newsletter of Kibbutz Barkai,* April 16, 1985. Translator unknown.

CHAPTER 22

Some Jewish Children Grow Up in Shadows

In recent years, a new chapter has been added to the Holocaust literature the experiences of Jewish children who lived in secret during the war. Yale historian Deborah Dwork estimates that there may have been as many as 200,000 Jewish children in hiding, assuming new identities to evade the Nazis. Some lived in monasteries or on farms, others in sewers, attics or forests. No more than half of them survived. Some were babies, pressed into the arms of Gentile neighbors as their parents were loaded on the deportation trains. Others were adopted by families who never revealed their true lineage. Some of them, said Dwork, are still children in hiding.

In 1939, when he was seven, Alexander Fischler, now a retired professor from the State University Center at Binghamton, was separated from his parents. He and his brother fled to France, where they spent two years at a Catholic school as hidden children until they were smuggled into Spain and eventually resettled in Palestine. It was ten years before Fischler was reunited with his mother. He never saw his father again.

"I was born in Czechoslovakia in 1931, so that automatically doomed me to be a hidden child since we didn't get out of Europe in time.

"I have very few memories of my father. He had a fabrics store, and my mother worked with him in the store. I was their second child.

Actually, there was going to be another one, but the war started and my mother aborted it. Things were just too horrific. So there were just the two of us, my brother, who was three and a half years older, and me. Most of my memories start with the war; at the time I was seven years old.

"First, we were forced to move out of the Sudetenland because Hitler claimed it as part of Germany. So we moved to Prague. The war was imminent, and my parents were trying to arrange for us all to emigrate to Australia. My brother and I flew to France in 1939, and we went to live with some cousins. The plan was that our parents would join us and from there we'd all go to Australia. But my parents never made it. Hitler occupied Czechoslovakia and my parents escaped to Poland. Then when the Germans took Poland, the first thing they did was they asked all male Jews between the ages of six and 60 to report to the police. And my father never came back. The word was that they had trucked them out of town and forced them to dig a trench and then machine-gunned them. So my mother never saw my father again. I never saw my father again.

"When the Germans occupied the southern part of France, our relatives, with whom we were staying, went into hiding. So we went into hiding, too. They found a Catholic school run by a teaching order of priests to take us. The only man who in the beginning knew who we were was the director of the school. We made an arrangement: Since our name, Fischler, is Germanic, what they did was tell us to pretend that we came from Alsace, which was right next to the German border. The only problem was that one day, one of the priests who was from Alsace came to us with a postcard from there. And I didn't recognize anything. But my brother, who was kind of clever, said, 'Oh, isn't that the city hall?' It looked like a city hall. So that's what he said. And it was all right. It made the transition.

"I knew I had to pass for a Catholic. No question about it. It was life and death. There were a lot of fascists around 'French' fascists and they would have been delighted to denounce anybody. So I became a choirboy.

"I don't think I looked very Jewish. There were many kids who looked as Jewish as I did. Also, by that time, I had lived in France for three and a half years. I'd gone to French schools. I knew everything French. There was no way to distinguish me from any other French kid.

"In the end, only three people in the school knew that we were Jewish: The director, who knew from the start; the officiating priest, because he had to understand why we went through confession rather rapidly and why we did not go to communion; and the discipline prefect. And none of them ever divulged it.

"We stayed until December 1943. The Nazis by then were rounding up Jews in France and sending them to concentration camps. They would block off streets in the center of town, where everybody congregated, and sort out Jews and immediately ship them off. So my relatives began making arrangements to find someone to smuggle us into Spain.

"All this time, I couldn't hear from my mother. We were completely out of touch. After my father was taken away, she found a Polish family that took her in as a maid. Her landlady, seeing how distraught she was, had taken pity on her and given my mother a (gentile's) birth certificate. So she was able to find this Polish family to take her in, and she survived with them during the war.

"We weren't reunited right away after the war. My mother tried first to save whatever we had left in Czechoslovakia. We had hidden bolts of cloth, silver, things like that with Czech families. My mother didn't know where anything was. She had no list. But when the people in this town heard Mrs. Fischler was back, they started arriving with a bolt of cloth under their arm, with a silver dish in their hands, one after another. And my mother said she didn't think anything was lost.

"In 1949, we were reunited in Israel. It was exactly ten years and two weeks since we had been separated. I was 17."

Source: Binghamton *Press and Sun-Bulletin,* December 4, 1991.

CHAPTER **23**

Epilogue

While the Holocaust ended 50 years ago, it is very important for today's young people to study it and learn lessons about history from the destruction of European Jews. The following essay was written in 1995 by a nine-year-old boy from Binghamton, Jeremy Levine-Murray, telling of his interest in the Holocaust. It makes for an appropriate epilogue to this collection of documents on Holocaust survivors and witnesses in the Triple Cities area.

Understanding the Past for a Better Future

I became interested in the Holocaust when I was in the second grade. I first learned about the Holocaust from my religious school teacher, Ilana Segal. I read books about people's accounts of their experiences. I couldn't believe how cruel human beings could be to other human beings. I couldn't believe that it was real. It sounded like an old fashioned horror story. I read more and discovered it was true.

I learned a great deal from reading different types of Holocaust books. My favorite book is *Daniel's Story.* Daniel experienced every bad thing that could happen to Jews at that time. I learned that it wasn't just one crazy man who created the Holocaust. Adolf Hitler wanted to take over the world (which was a classic act of stupidity). Since it was hard times in Germany (people out of jobs, etc.) the Germans needed an excuse for why they were messed up. So they followed Hitler and blamed the Jews, Gypsies and Communists. Jews suffered the most.

I realize that the Nazis had different types of concentration camps. Some were death camps and others were labor camps. Jews had to endure horrible conditions. It is hard to believe that people survived under these conditions.

I also learned that not all Germans were Nazis. Some helped Jews by hiding them, giving them food, or working against the Nazis. Some Jews also resisted. Take the Warsaw Ghetto. The Jews fought back against the Nazis. People did what they could to survive. Some Jews disagreed with other Jews over how to survive.

It must be hard for survivors to have to live with the memory of living in concentration camps. I wonder what they feel like when they take a shower and have that number on their arm like a branded cow. Once I wrote to Elie Wiesel asking him if he could send me stories that he heard when he was in Auschwitz. He wrote back to me. He suggested that I read his book, *Night.* He said it was the true account of his experiences as a boy in Auschwitz. He also thought I should read it along with my parents.

Learning about the Holocaust is important. For me, I learned about a part of Jewish history, a very painful part. I learned about the dark side of human beings. An understanding of the Holocaust gives an understanding of the importance of fighting against injustice and prejudice. As we live in difficult times, it is important that we do not blame others for our troubles. It is up to kids like me to keep alive the gruesome memory of the Holocaust so another Holocaust will not happen in the future to Jews and non-Jews alike. It is now our responsibility to struggle against injustice and prejudice, in all forms, against all people. This is important so that we can all live in a better world where people who have different skin color or a different religion or different political beliefs can live without fear of being treated unfairly.

Source: *Jeremy R. Levine-Murray, Temple Concord Religious School, Binghamton, NY, 1995.*

Temple Israel Holocaust Memorial Monument Vestal, NY
Photo by Steve Appel

Chronology of the Holocaust

January 30,1933	Hitler (b. 1889 in Braunau, Austria) appointed Chancellor of Germany
March 10, 1933	Dachau Concentration camp opened
April 1, 1933	Nazi Boycott
May 10, 1933	Burning of Jewish Books
September 15, 1935	Annexation of Austria
March 13, 1938	Nuremberg Racial Laws
November 9-10, 1938	Kristallnacht
November 15, 1938	Public Schools closed to Jewish children
September 1, 1939	Nazi Invasion of Poland
April 27, 1940	Auschwitz Concentration camp opened
September 29-30, 1941	Babi Yar (Kiev) 34,000 Jews executed by SS
December 7, 1941	Pearl Harbor. The United States enters WWII
January 20, 1942	Wannsee Conference (Final Solution)
February, 1942	Sinking of the Struma
July 6, 1942	Anne Frank (age 13) goes into hiding
April 19, 1943	Warsaw Ghetto Uprising begins
June 6, 1944	D-Day
July, 1944	Swedish diplomat, Raoul Wallenberg, sent to Hungary on rescue mission
January 27, 1945	Liberation of Auschwitz by Soviet troops
April 15, 1945	Bergen-Belsen Concentration camp liberated by British
May 8, 1945	V-E Day
November 29, 1945	Beginning of Nuremberg War Crimes Trials

Number of Victims

Country	Estimated Pre-Final Solution Population	Estimated Jewish Population Annihilated	Percent Population Annihilated
Poland	3,300,000	3,000,000	90
Baltic Countries	253,000	228,000	90
Germany/Austria	240,000	210,000	90
Protectorate	90,000	80,000	89
Slovakia	90,000	75,000	83
Greece	70,000	54,000	77
The Netherlands	140,000	105,000	75
Hungary	650,000	450,000	70
SSR White Russia	375,000	245,000	65
SSR Ukraine*	1,500,000	900,000	60
Belgium	65,000	40,000	60
Yugoslavia	43,000	26,000	60
Rumania	600,000	300,000	50
Norway	1,500	900	50
France	350,000	90,000	26
Bulgaria	64,000	14,000	22
Italy	40,000	8,000	20
Luxemberg	5,000	1,000	20
Russia (RSFSR)	975,000	107,000	11
Denmark	8,000	-	-
Finland	2,000	-	-
Total	8,861,800	5,933,900	67

* The Germans did not occupy all of the territory of this republic

Source: Lucy S. Dawidowicz, *The War Against the Jews*, 1975, pg. 403

–Glossary

AMERICAN JOINT DISTRIBUTION COMMITTEE (JDC) was founded in 1914 and is the principal American Jewish agency providing overseas relief to distressed Jewish communities. Also referred to as "The Joint," the JDC distributed over $78 million in aid during the Holocaust.

ANTI-SEMITISM is the dislike or fear of Jews or Judaism. Nazism seized on a virulent mode of racial anti-Semitism and made hatred of the Jewish people one its core ideological features.

ARAMAIC is an ancient language similar to Hebrew. It was spoken by Jews in the time of Jesus in Roman Palestine and is the principal language of the Talmud, the most important compilation of classical rabbinic writings (c. 200-500 CE).

AUSCHWITZ, located in southern Poland, was the largest complex of Nazi concentration and extermination camps, including the notorious Birkenau death camp. Over one million Jews were murdered at Auschwitz.

BABI YAR, a ravine near the Ukrainian city of Kiev where nearly 34,000 Jews were executed by Nazi storm troopers in two days, September 29 and 30,1941. Subsequent executions at the same location brought the total number of victims at Babi Yar to 100,000.

BERGEN-BELSEN, a concentration camp in northern Germany located near the city of Hanover was the first camp on the western front to be liberated by the Allies (April 15, 1945). Anne Frank died there one month prior to liberation.

CHASID or "a pious one" in Hebrew, is a member of one of several dozen East European Jewish religious sects. Known for their fervor, mysticism and devotion to dynastic "rebbes," the Chasidim (pl.) were among the chief victims of the Nazi war against the Jews.

CHEDER, literally "room" in Hebrew, refers to tiny elementary Hebrew schools for boys, especially in East Europe. Religious instruction and language training was provided by a "melamed" or a "Rebbe" (not to be confused with the dynastic leaders of Hasidic sects).

CHELMO, a Nazi extermination camp in western Poland near the city of Lodz. Over 360,000 Jews were murdered there. The camp was liberated by the Soviet Army in January, 1945; only two Jews survived.

CONCENTRATION CAMPS were mass detention centers originally created by the Nazis to quarantine a wide variety of people deemed "undesirable" by the Nazi state. While executions were carried out in concentration camps from their inception, their use for huge liquidation programs did not emerge until the beginning of 1942.

CREMATORIA are furnaces or complexes designed and used for burning human bodies. The Nazis installed industrial scale crematoria in many of the death camps as an "efficient" way of disposing of the millions of bodies of their victims.

DACHAU is a small village near Munich in southern Germany and the site of the first concentration camp. It became a model and training center for other, larger SS operations and a site for medical experimentation. Dachau was established in March, 1933 and was liberated on April 29, 1945 by American troops.

DISPLACED PERSONS, sometimes referred to as DPs, were among the survivors of the Holocaust and the ravages of World War II. Many of the Jewish DPs were quarantined in postwar allied "camps" and sought to resettle in Palestine despite the active objection of the British government.

EINSATZGRUPPEN, special mobile SS units dispatched to the eastern front in the wake of the Nazi's 1941 invasion of the Soviet Union. Organized into four sectors, the Einsatzgruppen organized mass executions and firing squads. See BABI YAR.

FASCISM is a dictatorial form of government which suppresses political opposition and favors private ownership of industry under the control of the central government. It is also associated with aggressive forms of nationalism, racism and glorifies war.

FINAL SOLUTION or "Endloesung" in German, refers to Nazi plans to exterminate the entire Jewish people. Used as early as 1939, the phrase "Final Solution" is often associated with the 1942 Wannsee Conference at which the decision was made by ranking Nazi officials to change methods from mass shootings (see BABI YAR and EINSATSGRUPPEN) to industrial sized gas chambers.

FOURTH LATERAN COUNCIL, an important turning point in the history of anti-Semitism, was summoned by Pope Innocent III in 1215. It compelled Jews and other non-Christians to wear distinctive clothing in public, prohibited Jews from holding public office and restricted Jewish economic activity.

GESTAPO or "Secret State Police" initially persecuted Jews and others in the Third Reich and subsequently played a critical role in implementing the FINAL SOLUTION. After the war, few leaders of the Gestapo were apprehended and brought to justice.

GHETTOS refers to quarantined urban areas. Historically connected to the anti-Jewish measures of the Counter Reformation, ghettos were widely established in pre-modern Europe as compulsory areas of Jewish settlement. Officially terminated by Napoleon and others, ghettos were reestablished by Nazis beginning in 1939 and were systematically and brutally liquidated by the Germans. In many of the ghettos, civilian Jewish paramilitary units were organized and fought valiantly. In subsequent usage, the term ghetto has gained a wider application.

HIAS or "Hebrew Immigrant Aid Society" was organized in New York in 1902 by merging a number of Jewish resettlement agencies. HIAS quickly emerged and remains the leading agency for Jewish immigrant resettlement and refugee assistance in the United States.

HINDENBURG, PAUL VON (1847-1934) was a leading German military and political leader. In 1932, he was reelected President of Germany but failed to uphold the Republic's constitution. He helped ally his followers with the Nazi party and appointed Hitler to the Reichschancellery. Following Hindenberg's death, Hitler consolidated his power and proclaimed himself Fuehrer.

HITLER, ADOLF (1889-1945) was the principal leader of Nazism and the person most responsible for the murder of six million Jews during the Holocaust. Born in Austria, Hitler was a World War I veteran who later became involved in extreme right wing politics. A hypnotic public speaker and vicious anti-Semite, he organized the Nazi party during the 1920s. After proclaiming himself Dictator in 1933, Hitler quickly expanded Germany's military capacity and in 1939 started World War II, the greatest military conflict in history, by invading Poland. In 1945, the Allies defeated Nazi Germany and demanded an unconditional surrender. Instead of facing capture and a war crimes trial, Hitler committed suicide in a bunker in Berlin. Hitler, it can be said without exaggeration, was the most evil man in world history.

HOLOCAUST or Greek for "burnt offering" refers to the systematic attempt of Nazi Germany to exterminate the entire Jewish people. In 12 years, between 1933 and 1945, the Nazis were responsible for the murder of six million Jews. However, they failed both to destroy the Jewish people and establish a 1,000 year Reich. The Hebrew word for Holocaust is "Shoah."

KADDISH is an important part of the Jewish worship service. Written mostly in ARAMAIC, it appears in several forms, most importantly as the "Mourners' Prayer" recited toward the end of Jewish services. Its ancient sound and special rhythm provide comfort and healing to those who recite it.

KAPO is a prisoner in charge of other inmates in a Nazi concentration camp. The exact origin of the word is unknown but may be related to the Italian word for "boss" (capo). Most Kapos were vicious people who followed the lead of their SS organizers. The term Kapo is associated with cruelty and exploitation.

KRISTALLNACHT, German for "Night of Broken Glass," marked a turning point in organized, public Nazi violence against Jews and Judaism in Germany. On November 9-10, 1938, the Nazis unleashed a wave of violence in Germany which resulted in the demolition of nearly every synagogue in the country, massive destruction of Jewish property and widespread arrests of German Jews. Kristallnacht marked the beginning of the end of German Jewish life.

MINYAN, Hebrew for "quorum," refers to the required number of people necessary to convene a Jewish prayer service. Traditionally, a minyan is made up of ten Jewish men. Most of the more modern branches of Judaism count women in the minyan as well.

NAZISM, the ideology of the National Socialist German Workers' Party (NSDAP), is a virulent and highly racist brand of FASCISM. Championed by ADOLF HITLER, Nazism dominated German and Austrian politics for 12 years, 1933-1945 and resulted in the deaths of tens of millions of people in Europe and North Africa. One of Nazism's foremost goals was the physical destruction of the Jewish people and eradication of Judaism. Nazism's best known symbol is the SWASTIKA.

NUREMBERG RACIAL LAWS were enacted by the Nazi government on September 15, 1935. They stripped German Jews of their citizenship, forbade marriages between Aryans (Germans) and Jews and required that the letter "J" be stamped on identity papers carried by Jews. The Nuremberg Laws became the foundation for extensive "legal" discrimination against Jews in Nazi Germany.

POGROM, the Russian word for "devastation," originally referred to organized attacks and massacres of Jews in the Czarist Empire around the turn-of-the-century. Today, the term is often used more broadly.

REICHSTAG, the lower house of the German Parliament during the Second Reich and the Weimar Republic. Following the election of March 1933, in which the Nazis won 44 percent of the total vote, they burned the Reichstag, consolidated their power and named HITLER dictator with absolute power.

RESISTANCE refers broadly to individual and organized civilian attempts in many sectors, Jewish and non-Jewish, to combat Nazism and preserve human dignity in occupied Europe. Jewish resistance also includes the partisan movement and other guerilla efforts in which Jews took up arms against the Nazis in the forests, ghettos and concentration camps. Many partisan units were also involved in rescue operations and, following the war, assisted Jewish emigration, especially to Palestine.

SHABBAT or **SHABBOS** is the Jewish "day of rest." Commemorating the creation of the world, the Jewish Sabbath begins on Friday night at sunset and continues for 24 hours. Traditionally, the Jewish Sabbath is inaugurated with blessings said at home, includes several services in the synagogue and is characterized by a total prohibition on work.

SWASTIKA, the principal symbol of NAZISM, consists of a cross with eight arms of equal length, each arm connected at a right angle, configured in a clockwise direction. Swastikas have been used in many cultures, extending back to prehistoric times. The term itself may be of Sanskrit origins and ironically means "well-being."

THERESIENSTADT or Terezin in Czech, is a town in Czechoslovakia (today, in the Czech Republic) in which the Nazis established a GHETTO in October 1941 for Jews from Western and Central Europe. The SS used it as a "model settlement" to deflect concerns about death camps and reports of Nazi atrocities. Long before liberation in May 1945 by the Soviet Army, Theresienstadt became a deportation center to extermination camps. Epidemics also ravaged the inmate population at Theresienstadt.

TREBLINKA was the site of one of main Nazi extermination centers. Over 750,000 Jews were murdered at Treblinka which is located in Poland, 62 miles northeast of Warsaw.

YIDDISH is a German-Jewish language which first emerged in Germany during the Middle Ages and was brought to Poland in the 14th century by Jewish immigrants invited to settle there by Casimir, the Polish king. Written in Hebrew, Yiddish has several dialects, no standard spelling system and became the linguistic base for the rich Jewish cultural life of Eastern Europe often referred to as Yiddishkeit. The vast majority of American Jews are descendants of Yiddish speaking immigrants.

YOM KIPPUR or the Day of Atonement is the most sacred day of the year for Jews. Yom Kippur falls on the tenth day of the first month in the Jewish calendar (Tishri). Its customs includes a total 24 hour fast (no food or drinks for everyone over age 13), the prohibition of all work, extensive worship services and ends with the dramatic sounding of the ram's horn or Shofar.

ZIONISM is a modern Jewish nationalist movement which resulted in the creation of the State of Israel in 1948, the revival of the Hebrew language and the ingathering of over four million Jews to the land of Israel, the ancient cradle of the Jewish people. Zionism seeks both to provide for the safety of the Jewish people and the revival of Jewish culture. It is derived from a more traditional religious belief in restorationism. The word "Zion" is a poetic term for Israel and Jerusalem.

Select Bibliography

Berkovits, Eliezer. *Faith After the Holocaust.* New York, 1973.

Dawidowicz, Lucy S. *A Holocaust Reader.* New York, 1976.

Dawidowicz, Lucy S. *The War Against the Jews, 1933-1945.* New York, 1975.

Frank, Anne. *The Diary of a Young Girl,* 1995.

Friesel, Eyatan. *Atlas of Modern Jewish History.* New York, 1990.

Friedlander, Albert H., ed. *Out of the Whirlwind: A Reader of Holocaust Literature.* Garden City, NY. 1968.

Goldhagen, Daniel. *Hitler's Willing Executioners: Ordinary Germans and The Holocaust.* New York, 1996

Hilberg, Raul. *The Destruction of European Jews.* New York, 1961.

Katz, Steven T., *The Holocaust in Historical Context.* New York, 1994.

Lipstadt, Deborah. *Denying the Holocaust: The Growing Assault on Truth and Memory.* New York, 1994.

Read, Anthony and David Fisher. *Kristallnacht: The Unleashing of the Holocaust.* New York, 1989.

Schwartz-Bart, Andre. *Last of the Just.* 1961.

Trunk, Isaiah. *Judenrat: The Jewish Councils in Eastern Europe Nazi Occupation.* New York, 1972.

Weinrich, Max. *Hitler's Professors: The Part of Scholarship in Germany's Crimes Against the Jewish People.* New York, 1946.

Wiesel, Elie. *Night.* 1960.

–Index

About the Editors

RABBI LANCE J. SUSSMAN is spiritual leader of Temple Concord in Binghamton, New York and Associate Professor of American Jewish History, Department of History, Binghamton University (SUNY). He is author of *Beyond the Catskills,* a history of the Binghamton Jewish community and *Isaac Leeser and the Making of American Judaism.* Rabbi Sussman and his wife, Liz, live in Endwell with their five children.

MARY ROSE is a former librarian of Temple Concord and a trustee of the synagogue. She is a registered nurse and works in the Birthing Center unit at Lourdes Hospital in Binghamton. She and her husband, Matthew, and their two children live in Binghamton. *In Our Midst* is Mary Rose's first book.

STEVEN T. KATZ is one of the world's leading Holocaust experts. A highly prolific author, his latest book, *The Holocaust in Historical Context* a massive, comparative study of genocide, has been widely acclaimed as a masterpiece of modern historical research. Professor Katz has taught at many leading universities including Harvard, Dartmouth and Cornell. He recently accepted a new teaching position at Boston University. Professor Katz and his wife, Rika, and three children, lived in Binghamton for 12 years, 1984-1996.